Table of Contents

Table of Contents

Table of Contents

to

Sherri Brady
in whom I see and have experienced God's grace.

*All Scripture is God-breathed and is useful
for teaching, rebuking, correcting and training
in righteousness, so that the man of God may
be thoroughly equipped for every good work.*
2 Timothy 3:16-17 (NIV)

Introduction

People have lots of questions about what the Bible teaches, but very little time. *Pocket Theology* is written to provide answers for those on the go. Whether you are a non-Christian, wanting to simply learn more about what the Bible teaches, a Christian parent wanting to be better prepared to answer the questions your children are asking, or a leader within the church needing a quick reference guide to biblical theology, this book is for you.

This book is designed to serve as a quick reference tool, offering both a concise theological summary on a broad range of topics, as well as Scripture references for those who want to do further study. Sprinkled throughout the book, I have also included some short answers to some of the most common questions that people ask about the Christian faith. Questions like: "Why are there so many different versions of the Bible?" "What are we to make of the fact that there are so many different Christian denominations?" and "What exactly is the gospel?" These explanations are not exhaustive, but will provide enough information for most people to better understand the issues at hand. I have also included a glossary of theological terms, which will make ancient terms more accessible.

Finally, this book is also written for those working to care for others spiritually. As a pastor, I am reminded daily that shepherds don't grow the grass. They just point to it. This means that anytime we are caring for others spiritually our job is to simply point to the truth of God's Word. Ultimately it is only the truth of God's Word that satisfies, sustains, strengthens, enlightens, delivers, heals, comforts, convicts, rebukes, encourages and trains us in righteousness. It is tempting to offer our own words of wisdom when guiding others, or the popular psychology of the day, but the greatest need we all have is to hear the truth of God's Word. It is the Scripture that is "useful," because it is the Scripture that is "God-breathed."

It is my prayer that this book is a blessing.

Sincerely,
Kelly Brady

Making the most of this book...

Table of Contents
The topics listed in the table of contents are alphabetical. Taking a moment to familiarize yourself with these topics will help in the days ahead as you are looking for quick answers to your questions.

Theological Statements
The aim of this book is to provide answers from the Bible. Toward that end there are short theological statements offered, with Scriptural references throughout the book. The theological statements are in "bold" type. While these theological statements are certainly not all that can be said on the topic being addressed, they are offered as a beginning point.

Scripture References
While each Scripture is coupled with a theological statement, there are many theological statements which are not offered, which could be made about the Scripture referenced. In fact, on any of the Scripture references provided, virtually dozens of theological truths could be gleaned. For this reason, the theological statements offered are not meant to be exhaustive, but are introductory and foundational. Further, because each of the passages of Scripture referenced are lifted out of their biblical context, in order to be placed within the book, they will in some cases be difficult to understand without going to the passage and reading them in context.

Glossary
It would be impossible to provide a "pocket-sized" quick reference guide that covers every possible theological topic. For this reason, a glossary of theological words is offered at the back of the book. You will note that for most of the words, not only has a definition been provided but also a Scripture reference that will help with understanding.

Prayer
Anytime we are wanting to understand the teachings of Scripture, we must begin with prayer. Apart from God opening our minds to understand the words of Scripture, we are without hope (Luke 24:45). But as we diligently seek to know the truths of Scripture, he is eager to make himself known to us (Matthew 7:7-8).

Abortion

Debate over whether abortion is murder, and thus a breaking of the sixth commandment (Exodus 20:13), hinges on identifying when life begins. On this issue, Scripture repeatedly affirms God's interaction with people before birth, which demonstrates that life begins in the womb.

Abortion is murder because we are known by God in the womb.

"Before I formed you in the womb I knew you, and before you were born I consecrated you; I have appointed you a prophet to the nations."
Jeremiah 1:5 (NASB)

For You formed my inward parts; You wove me in my mother's womb. My frame was not hidden from You, when I was made in secret, and skillfully wrought in the depths of the earth.
Psalms 139:13, 15 (NASB)

But when he had considered this, behold, an angel of the Lord appeared to him in a dream, saying, "Joseph, son of David, do not be afraid to take Mary as your wife; for the Child who has been conceived in her is of the Holy Spirit.
Matthew 1:20 (NASB)

Abortion is murder because being sinful at conception implies personal responsibility, which denotes personhood.

Surely I was sinful at birth, sinful from the time my mother conceived me. Psalm 51:6 (NIV)

Abortion is murder in that the Law prescribed capital punishment for those causing abortion.

"If men struggle with each other and strike a woman with child so that she gives birth prematurely, yet there is no injury, he shall surely be fined as the woman's husband may demand of him, and he shall pay as the judges decide. "But if there is any further injury, then you shall appoint as a penalty life for life, eye for eye, tooth for tooth, hand for hand, foot for foot, burn for burn, wound for wound, bruise for bruise. Exodus 21:22-25 (NASB)

13

Addiction

Addiction, whether psychological or physical, is common within our modern culture. However, a life of addiction is contrary to the life of freedom from sin we are offered through the power of Christ's resurrection.

Addiction is to be mastered by something that is not beneficial.
All things are lawful for me, but not all things are profitable. All things are lawful for me, but I will not be mastered by anything.
1 Corinthians 6:12 (NASB)

Addiction is taught by false teachers who promise freedom but live as slaves themselves.
For speaking out arrogant words of vanity they entice by fleshly desires, by sensuality, those who barely escape from the ones who live in error, promising them freedom while they themselves are slaves of corruption; for by what a man is overcome, by this he is enslaved.
2 Peter 2:18-19 (NASB)

Addiction is a failure to honor God with the body.
Food is for the stomach and the stomach is for food, but God will do away with both of them Yet the body is not for immorality, but for the Lord, and the Lord is for the body. *1 Corinthians 6:13 (NASB)*

Addiction is a thankless posture of abusing God's good creation.
For everything created by God is good, and nothing is to be rejected if it is received with gratitude; for it is sanctified by means of the word of God and prayer. *1 Timothy 4:4 (NASB)*

Addiction is overcome through him (Jesus) who strengthens us.
I know how to get along with humble means, and I also know how to live in prosperity; in any and every circumstance I have learned the secret of being filled and going hungry, both of having abundance and suffering need. I can do all things through Him who strengthens me.
Philippians 4:12-13 (ESV)

Angels

Angels are created beings who serve God's purposes and people.
Are they not all ministering spirits sent out to serve for the sake of those who are to inherit salvation? Hebrews 1:14 (ESV)

See that you do not despise one of these little ones. For I tell you that in heaven their angels always see the face of my Father who is in heaven. Matthew 18:10 (ESV)

Angels appear to people, carry messages and defend God's people.
And the angel said to them, "Fear not, for behold, I bring you good news of great joy that will be for all the people." Luke 2:10 (ESV)

Do not neglect to show hospitality to strangers, for thereby some have entertained angels unawares. Hebrews 13:2 (ESV)

But when the archangel Michael, contending with the devil, was disputing about the body of Moses, he did not presume to pronounce a blasphemous judgment, but said, "The Lord rebuke you." Jude 9 (ESV)

While I was speaking in prayer, the man Gabriel, whom I had seen in the vision at the first, came to me in swift flight at the time of the evening sacrifice. He made me understand, speaking with me and saying, "O Daniel, I have now come out to give you insight and understanding." Daniel 9:21-22 (ESV)

And behold, an angel of the Lord stood next to him, and a light shone in the cell. He struck Peter on the side and woke him, saying, "Get up quickly." And the chains fell off his hands. Acts 12:7 (ESV)

Angels are sent to carry out God's judgment.
Immediately an angel of the Lord struck him down, because he did not give God the glory, and he was eaten by worms and breathed his last. Acts 12:23 (ESV)

Angels rebelled in some instances and received God's judgment.
And the angels who did not stay within their own position of authority, but left their proper dwelling, he has kept in eternal chains under gloomy darkness until the judgment of the great day. Jude 1:6 (ESV)

Anointing with Oil

It is common in some Christian denominations to put a little bit of oil on the forehead of those receiving prayer for healing. While this is a centuries old tradition, it is important to understand that there is no special power in the oil itself. The power for healing comes from God who blesses our obedience as we act in faith. While a strange practice from our modern perspective, anointing someone with oil is opportunity to exercise our faith, acting obediently on God's Word. And without faith we know that it is impossible to please God (Hebrews 11:6).

Anointing oil was used in the Old Testament to consecrate priests.
"Then you shall take the anointing oil and pour it on his head and anoint him. "You shall bring his sons and put tunics on them."
Exodus 29:7-8 (NASB)

Anointing oil was used in the Old Testament with sacrifices.
"Whatever is needed, both young bulls, rams, and lambs for a burnt offering to the God of heaven, and wheat, salt, wine and anointing oil, as the priests in Jerusalem request, it is to be given to them daily without fail, that they may offer acceptable sacrifices to the God of heaven and pray for the life of the king and his sons. Ezra 6:9-10 (NASB)

Anointing with oil was practiced by the disciples in healing.
They went out and preached that men should repent. And they were casting out many demons and were anointing with oil many sick people and healing them. Mark 6:12-13 (NASB)

Anointing with oil was commanded in the book of James.
Is any one of you sick? He should call the elders of the church to pray over him and anoint him with oil in the name of the Lord. And the prayer offered in faith will make the sick person well; the Lord will raise him up. If he has sinned, he will be forgiven.
James 5:14-15 (NIV)

Anxiety

Anxiety is an indication that we are not yet perfected in God's love.
There is no fear in love, but perfect love casts out fear. For fear has to do with punishment, and whoever fears has not been perfected in love.
1 John 4:8 (ESV)

Anxiety is an opportunity to pray and know God's peace.
Do not be anxious about anything, but in everything by prayer and supplication with thanksgiving let your requests be made known to God. And the peace of God, which surpasses all understanding, will guard your hearts and your minds in Christ Jesus. Philippians 4:6-7 (ESV)

Anxiety can be a distraction from what is important.
And he said to his disciples, "Therefore I tell you, do not be anxious about your life, what you will eat, nor about your body, what you will put on. For life is more than food, and the body more than clothing. Luke 12:22-23 (ESV)

But the Lord answered her, "Martha, Martha, you are anxious and troubled about many things, but one thing is necessary. Mary has chosen the good portion, which will not be taken away from her." Luke 10:41-42 (ESV)

Anxiety does not add to our control over life.
Consider the ravens: they neither sow nor reap, they have neither storehouse nor barn, and yet God feeds them. Of how much more value are you than the birds! And which of you by being anxious can add a single hour to his span of life? If then you are not able to do as small a thing as that, why are you anxious about the rest? Consider the lilies, how they grow: they neither toil nor spin, yet I tell you, even Solomon in all his glory was not arrayed like one of these. But if God so clothes the grass, which is alive in the field today, and tomorrow is thrown into the oven, how much more will he clothe you, O you of little faith! Luke 12:24-28 (ESV)

Apologetics

The word "apologetics" comes from the Greek word *apologia*, which means "to make a verbal defense" or to offer reasons for a belief. The Apostle Peter writes that we are to be prepared to answer everyone who asks for the "reason" (apologia) for the hope we have in Jesus Christ (1 Peter 3:15).

Apologetics is a work for which we are to be prepared and we are to do in gentleness and respect.
But in your hearts set apart Christ as Lord. Always be prepared to give an answer to everyone who asks you to give the reason for the hope that you have. But do this with gentleness and respect, keeping a clear conscience, so that those who speak maliciously against your good behavior in Christ may be ashamed of their slander.
1 Peter 3:15-16 (NIV)

Doing apologetics, Paul noted how many, who were still living at that time, saw Jesus resurrected.
After that, he appeared to more than five hundred of the brothers at the same time, most of whom are still living, though some have fallen asleep. Then he appeared to James, then to all the apostles, and last of all he appeared to me also, as to one abnormally born.
1 Corinthians 15:6-8 (NIV)

The work of apologetics implies that the Christian faith is reasonable—that is to say that there are rational explanations for what we believe. However, becoming a Christian will always require a leap of faith. For example, although we are able to rationally demonstrate that the Bible is a trustworthy and historically accurate source of information, we will never be able to prove that it is the inspired Word of God. Believing that the Bible is inspired is a tenet of faith, believing that it is historically reliable is deduction based upon evidence.

Apologetics leads to faith as the Holy Spirit convinces people.
The man without the Spirit does not accept the things that come from the Spirit of God, for they are foolishness to him, and he cannot understand them, because they are spiritually discerned.
1 Corinthians 2:14 (NIV)

Arminianism

Arminianism is the theological system of James Arminius (1560-1609). Although living during the Protestant Reformation, Arminius wrote his theology not in response to the teachings of the Roman Catholic church, but rather in response to some of the most influential leaders within the Reformation, most notably John Calvin. While holding many theological beliefs in common with John Calvin, such as the belief that all humans are born sinful and that Scripture is inspired by God and inerrant in the original manuscripts, he differed with Calvin on the role of humanity in the work of salvation.

Arminianism teaches that salvation is the result of God's predestination of those whom he foreknew would freely accept the atonement for sin provided through Jesus Christ's death. This differs from Calvinism, which purports that man's free will does not play a role in salvation, but rather that in God's sovereignty he saves, through his irresistible grace, only those whom he chooses.

In response to Calvinism, the followers of Arminius offered five points of protest.

Universal Prevenient Grace. This grace given by God, overcomes the effects of sin and provides the freedom needed to either accept or reject salvation offered through Jesus Christ.

Conditional Election. God elects to save only those whom he foreknew would accept Jesus Christ as Savior.

Unlimited Atonement. Christ died for all people, but those who are saved are only those whom God foreknew would freely choose to believe.

Resistible Grace. God never forces his will upon mankind, but all are free to reject or accept the forgiveness offered in Jesus.

Uncertainty of Perseverance. Although the grace and power needed to persevere are available to all who believe in Christ, salvation can be lost by those who fail to persevere in the faith.

While it should be noted that not all who identify with Arminianism affirm each of these five points, Arminianism is best known for its affirmation of man's will, which is thought to be freely exercised in the process of salvation.

The Methodist, Wesleyan, Assembly of God and Pentecostal denominations are Arminian in their theology, as well as many independent and non-denominational, and Baptist churches.

Baptism

The mode of baptism, whether sprinkling or immersion, varies between denominations. However, the practice of baptism was modeled and commanded by Jesus.

Baptism was modeled by Jesus.
Then Jesus arrived from Galilee at the Jordan coming to John, to be baptized by him. Matthew 3:13 (NASB)

Baptism was commanded by Jesus.
Go therefore and make disciples of all the nations, baptizing them in the name of the Father and the Son and the Holy Spirit.
Matthew 28:19 (NASB)

Baptism was practiced by the early church.
Peter replied, "Repent and be baptized, every one of you, in the name of Jesus Christ for the forgiveness of your sins. And you will receive the gift of the Holy Spirit. Acts 2:38 (NIV)

Baptism is a way to identify with Jesus' death and resurrection.
Or do you not know that all of us who have been baptized into Christ Jesus have been baptized into His death? Therefore we have been buried with Him through baptism into death, so that as Christ was raised from the dead through the glory of the Father, so we too might walk in newness of life. For if we have become united with Him in the likeness of His death, certainly we shall also be in the likeness of His resurrection. Romans 6:3-5 (NASB)

Baptism is a symbol of God's deliverance from sin and death.
In it only a few people, eight in all, were saved through water, and this water symbolizes baptism that now saves you also—not the removal of dirt from the body but the pledge of a good conscience toward God. It saves you by the resurrection of Jesus Christ, who has gone into heaven and is at God's right hand—with angels, authorities and powers in submission to him. 1 Peter 3:20-22 (NIV)

Born Again

"Born again" is the phrase that best describes the beginning of the process of salvation. Jesus said "you must be born again" (John 3:7). To be born again is to be made spiritually alive from the dead state into which we were all born as infants (Ephesians 2:1-4).

Being born again is a requirement for entering heaven.
Jesus answered him, "Truly, truly, I say to you, unless one is born again he cannot see the kingdom of God." John 3:3 (ESV)

Being born again is to be reborn by God's Spirit.
That which is born of the flesh is flesh, and that which is born of the Spirit is spirit. John 3:6 (ESV)

Being born again is granted to any who believe in Jesus' name.
But to all who did receive him, who believed in his name, he gave the right to become children of God. John 1:12 (ESV)

Being born again is brought by the will of God, not man.
Who were born, not of blood nor of the will of the flesh nor of the will of man, but of God. John 1:13 (ESV)

Being born again gives us the power to stop practicing sin.
No one born of God makes a practice of sinning, for God's seed abides in him, and he cannot keep on sinning because he has been born of God. 1 John 3:9 (ESV)

Being born again provides the power to overcome sin in the world.
For everyone who has been born of God overcomes the world. And this is the victory that has overcome the world— our faith.
1 John 5:4 (ESV)

Being born again provides protection from the evil one.
We know that everyone who has been born of God does not keep on sinning, but he who was born of God protects him, and the evil one does not touch him. 1 John 5:18 (ESV)

Calvinism

Calvinism is the theological system associated with John Calvin (1509-1564). John Calvin was a leader in the Protestant Reformation, the movement to reform the Roman Catholic church. His most famous theological work is *Institutes of the Christian Religion*.

Calvinism is synonymous with Reformed Protestant theology and is often nicknamed Covenant theology, because of its emphasis on God's gracious work to save by establishing a covenant through Jesus Christ's blood. In this way Calvinism emphasizes God's actions to save, rather than man's will to be saved or man's works of salvation.

Calvinism is often contrasted with Arminianism and the five main theological points of Calvinism are most often referred to by the acrostic TULIP. They are:

Total Depravity. Born into sin (Psalm 51:5; Ephesians 2:1-4), a condition characterized by a corrupted mind, body and will, sinfulness is the human condition. Originating with the first humans, Adam and Eve, sin is passed to all at conception (Romans 5:12-17). While this does not mean that humans are as depraved as we could be, it does mean that we are unable to act without sin's influence, and thus radically corrupted and unable to earn God's favor.

Unconditional Election. God has chosen those whom he wanted to save, based solely upon his will, and apart from any human merit or action (Romans 9:15, 21; Ephesians 1:4-8).

Limited Atonement. Christ's sacrificial death provides atonement for the sins of only those God has unconditionally elected (John 17:9, Ephesians 5:25).

Irresistible Grace. All whom God has unconditionally elected will respond to the offer of salvation (John 6:37, 44).

Perseverance of the Saints. All who are saved by God's grace will persevere though faith to receive eternal life (John 6:39; Romans 8:30).

Calvinism is historically embraced by the Reformed and Presbyterian denominations. There are also many Baptist, Congregational and independent churches that embrace Calvinism.

Church

The Church is the community of all who have saving faith in Jesus Christ throughout all time (Hebrews 12:1). The Church is both local and global, as well as universal, stretching throughout time and space. Locally, church is any gathering of two or more Christians for the purpose of worship (Mathew 18:20).

The Church is the body of Christ, of which he is the head.
And God placed all things under his feet and appointed him to be head over everything for the church, which is his body, the fullness of him who fills everything in every way. Ephesians 1:22-23 (NIV)

The Church is God's family and dwelling place.
So then you are no longer strangers and aliens, but you are fellow citizens with the saints, and are of God's household, having been built on the foundation of the apostles and prophets, Christ Jesus Himself being the corner stone, in whom the whole building, being fitted together, is growing into a holy temple in the Lord, in whom you also are being built together into a dwelling of God in the Spirit.
Ephesians 2:19-22 (NASB)

The Church is the bride of Christ.
Husbands, love your wives, just as Christ loved the church and gave himself up for her to make her holy, cleansing her by the washing with water through the word, and to present her to himself as a radiant church, without stain or wrinkle or any other blemish, but holy and blameless. Ephesians 5:25-27 (NIV)

The Church has been given authority and power by Jesus.
"I also say to you that you are Peter, and upon this rock I will build My church; and the gates of Hades will not overpower it. "I will give you the keys of the kingdom of heaven; and whatever you bind on earth shall have been bound in heaven, and whatever you loose on earth shall have been loosed in heaven." Matthew 16:18-19 (NASB)

The Church is the pillar and foundation of truth in the world.
If I am delayed, you will know how people ought to conduct themselves in God's household, which is the church of the living God, the pillar and foundation of the truth. 1 Timothy 3:15 (NIV)

Continued———▶

Church

The Church grows as the Lord adds to those being saved.

Day by day continuing with one mind in the temple, and breaking bread from house to house, they were taking their meals together with gladness and sincerity of heart, praising God and having favor with all the people. And the Lord was adding to their number day by day those who were being saved. Acts 2:46-47 (NASB)

The Church is God's means for displaying his wisdom.

His intent was that now, through the church, the manifold wisdom of God should be made known to the rulers and authorities in the heavenly realms, according to his eternal purpose which he accomplished in Christ Jesus our Lord. Ephesians 3:10-11 (NIV)

The Church is headed by Christ and it is to submit to Christ.

He is before all things, and in Him all things hold together. He is also head of the body, the church; and He is the beginning, the firstborn from the dead, so that He Himself will come to have first place in everything. Colossians 1:17-18 (NASB)

The Church gathering is not to be forsaken.

Let us not give up meeting together, as some are in the habit of doing, but let us encourage one another—and all the more as you see the Day approaching. Hebrews 10:25 (NIV)

The Church is to prepare one another for judgment.

Let us not give up meeting together, as some are in the habit of doing, but let us encourage one another—and all the more as you see the Day approaching. Hebrews 10:25 (NIV)

Circumcision

Circumcision is the removal of foreskin from the penis. Jewish males were to be circumcised eight days after birth. Circumcision was the sign of the covenant between God and the Jewish people (Genesis 17:10-11). Considering the *placement* of this symbol on the body we can gain some understanding of its significance.

God's commitment in the Old Testament covenant was to bless all the nations of the world through Abraham's descendents (Genesis 22:18). Thus, being circumcised served as a physical reminder of this promise. Ultimately, the promise to bless all the nations of the world has been fulfilled through Jesus Christ, one of Abraham's descendents, which is why both Matthew's and Luke's gospel trace Jesus' genealogy back to Abraham.

For the Jewish community, circumcision was the external sign of one's identity and hope in the promises of God to Abaham. It was the God-given symbol for all those trusting in God's promises, and the Apostle Paul draws a direct link between the ancient symbol of circumcision and the New Testament symbol of baptism. Paul writes:

In Christ you were also circumcised, in the putting off of the sinful nature, not with a circumcision done by the hands of men but with the circumcision done by Christ, having been buried with him in baptism and raised with him through your faith in the power of God, who raised him from the dead.
Colossians 2:11-12 (NIV)

Now that Jesus Christ has come circumcision is no longer needed. The old covenant with the Jewish people has been replaced by the new covenant in Jesus Christ (Ephesians 2:11-16), and the outward sign of the new covenant is baptism, the symbol that one's identity and hope in the promises of God to save through Jesus Christ. Like circumcision, baptism is an evidence of our trust in God to fulfill his promises.

There was some disagreement among the earliest Christians about whether circumcision was to continue as a symbol for God's new covenant people. But Paul settled the argument writing:

Look: I, Paul, say to you that if you accept circumcision, Christ will be of no advantage to you. I testify again to every man who accepts circumcision that he is obligated to keep the whole law. Galatians 5:2-3 (ESV)

Communion

Communion is the meal of remembrance, established by Jesus on the night before his death. Its purpose is primarily for remembering, but also proclaiming, his death as a sacrifice for the forgiveness of sin. As a meal of remembrance Communion is linked to the Jewish meal of remembrance known as the Passover (Exodus11). Jesus' shed blood, which is celebrated in the cup of the Communion meal, is described as a type of Passover sacrifice (1 Corinthians 5:7).

Communion was instituted by Jesus on the night of his death.

And he took bread, gave thanks and broke it, and gave it to them, saying, "This is my body given for you; do this in remembrance of me." In the same way, after the supper he took the cup, saying, "This cup is the new covenant in my blood, which is poured out for you.
Luke 22:19-20 (NIV)

Communion is a symbol of Jesus' shed blood and broken body.

For I received from the Lord that which I also delivered to you, that the Lord Jesus in the night in which He was betrayed took bread; and when He had given thanks, He broke it and said, "This is My body, which is for you; do this in remembrance of Me." In the same way He took the cup also after supper, saying, "This cup is the new covenant in My blood; do this, as often as you drink it, in remembrance of Me." For as often as you eat this bread and drink the cup, you proclaim the Lord's death until He comes. 1 Corinthians 11:23-26 (NASB)

Communion is a means for proclaiming the Lord's death.

For whenever you eat this bread and drink this cup, you proclaim the Lord's death until he comes. 1 Corinthians 11:26 (NIV)

Communion is to be taken only after self-examination.

Therefore whoever eats the bread or drinks the cup of the Lord in an unworthy manner, shall be guilty of the body and the blood of the Lord. But a man must examine himself, and in so doing he is to eat of the bread and drink of the cup. For he who eats and drinks, eats and drinks judgment to himself if he does not judge the body rightly.
1 Corinthians 11:27-29 (NASB)

Confession of Sin

Confession of sin includes either the listing of specific sins or the admission of one's awareness of sinfulness in general.

Confession of sin is necessary for God's forgiveness.
I acknowledged my sin to you, and I did not cover my iniquity; I said, "I will confess my transgressions to the LORD," and you forgave the iniquity of my sin. Psalm 32:5 (ESV)

Whoever conceals his transgressions will not prosper, but he who confesses and forsakes them will obtain mercy. Proverbs 28:13 (ESV)

If we confess our sins, he is faithful and just to forgive us our sins and to cleanse us from all unrighteousness. 1 John 1:9 (ESV)

Confession of sin accompanied John the Baptist's ministry.
Then Jerusalem and all Judea and all the region about the Jordan were going out to him, and they were baptized by him in the river Jordan, confessing their sins. Matthew 3:5-6 (ESV)

Confession of sin accompanied repentance leading to salvation.
Also many of those who were now believers came, confessing and divulging their practices. Acts 19:18 (ESV)

Confession of sin to one another is to be a part of healing prayer.
Therefore, confess your sins to one another and pray for one another, that you may be healed. The prayer of a righteous person has great power as it is working. James 5:16 (ESV)

Confession of sin takes precedence over worship.
Therefore if you are presenting your offering at the altar, and there remember that your brother has something against you, leave your offering there before the altar and go; first be reconciled to your brother, and then come and present your offering. Matthew 5:23-24 (NASB)

Confessing of sin bring God's compassion upon us.
He who conceals his transgressions will not prosper, but he who confesses and forsakes them will find compassion. Proverbs 28:13 (NASB)

27

Cults

A cult is typically defined as a group whose beliefs and/or actions depart significantly from the theological teachings of historic Christianity. The Apostle Paul predicted these types of groups would come and wrote to warn pastor Timothy.

But the Spirit explicitly says that in later times some will fall away from the faith, paying attention to deceitful spirits and doctrines of demons, by means of the hypocrisy of liars seared in their own conscience as with a branding iron.
1 Timothy 4:1-2 (NASB)

For the time will come when men will not put up with sound doctrine. Instead, to suit their own desires, they will gather around them a great number of teachers to say what their itching ears want to hear. They will turn their ears away from the truth and turn aside to myths.
2 Timothy 4:3-4 (NIV)

Cults are often distinguished from other world religions, in that they twist Christian theology, whether only in part or in whole. Rather than altogether rejecting the claims of Christianity, as other major world religions do, cults will adopt a portion of Christian theology making select changes to important aspects of essential beliefs, all the while claiming to be Christian.

Some essential teachings that are most often twisted by cults are: the doctrine of the Trinity, the role and relationship of the Holy Spirit within the Trinity, the deity of Jesus Christ, the bodily death and resurrection of Jesus Christ, and the immortality of the human soul.

For example, many cults will accept Jesus as a great teacher, but reject his claim to deity. In their attempt to make this claim fit with the teachings of Scripture they will change subtle aspects of the biblical text. This is common in John 1:1, which is often translated by cultists as "and the Word was "a" God," rather than the accepted and grammatically accurate translation "and the Word was God."

Some of the most recognized cults include: The Way International, Unification Church (Moonies), Hare Krishna, Mormonism (Latter Day Saints), and Jehovah's Witnesses.

Death

Death is the destiny of all and we should live with this awareness.
It is better to go to a house of mourning than to go to a house of feasting, for death is the destiny of every man; the living should take this to heart. Ecclesiastes 7:2 (NIV)

Death brings believers immediately into God's presence.
Jesus answered him, "I tell you the truth, today you will be with me in paradise." Luke 23:43 (NIV)

We are confident, I say, and would prefer to be away from the body and at home with the Lord. 2 Corinthians 5:8 (NIV)

Death is the result of sin, but Jesus provides life.
For the wages of sin is death, but the gift of God is eternal life in Christ Jesus our Lord. Romans 6:23 (NIV)

So then as through one transgression there resulted condemnation to all men, even so through one act of righteousness there resulted justification of life to all men. Romans 5:18 (NASB)

Death is a gain for Christians, as they are immediately with Christ.
For to me, to live is Christ and to die is gain. If I am to go on living in the body, this will mean fruitful labor for me. Yet what shall I choose? I do not know! I am torn between the two: I desire to depart and be with Christ, which is better by far; but it is more necessary for you that I remain in the body. Philippians 1:21-24 (NIV)

Death can be the result of obedience to God's commands.
Do not be afraid of what you are about to suffer. I tell you, the devil will put some of you in prison to test you, and you will suffer persecution for ten days. Be faithful, even to the point of death, and I will give you the crown of life. Revelation 2:10 (NIV)

Death is not to be feared by those trusting in Jesus for salvation.
Even though I walk through the valley of the shadow of death, I fear no evil, for You are with me; Your rod and Your staff, they comfort me. Psalm 23:4 (NASB)

Demons and Exorcism

Demons are fallen angels, evil spirits working with Satan. "Exorcism" is the term used for removing evil spirits from people. Exorcism is needed when a demon is residing in a person (Mark 5:15). Christians cannot be "possessed" (i.e. owned) by a demon, because we are children of God and receive the Holy Spirit when we are born again (1 John 3:10, 1 Corinthians 6:19). However, there are biblical examples of Christians being significantly influenced by demonic forces.

Peter rebukes Ananias saying, "how is it that Satan has so filled your heart that you have lied to the Holy Spirit" (Acts 5:3). Simon the Sorcerer is described as "captive to sin" (Acts 8:23). We open ourselves to demonic influence through sinful activities. For this reason, James tells us to "resist the devil and he will flee from us" (James 4:7), and Paul tells us to "stay in step with the Spirit" (Galatians 5:25). Activities such as: séances, Ouija boards, tarot cards, fortune tellers and witchcraft may uniquely open us to demonic influence. These types of occult activities were prohibited in the Old Testament (Deuteronomy 18:10,14). And there is one example of a fortune teller having an evil spirit (Acts 16:16).

Demons are rebellious angels, who are under God's judgment.
And the angels who did not stay within their own position of authority, but left their proper dwelling, he has kept in eternal chains under gloomy darkness until the judgment of the great day. Jude 1:6 (ESV)

For if God did not spare angels when they sinned, but cast them into hell and committed them to chains of gloomy darkness to be kept until the judgment; then the Lord knows how to rescue the godly from trials, and to keep the unrighteous under punishment until the day of judgment, and especially those who indulge in the lust of defiling passion and despise authority. 2 Peter 2:4,9-10 (ESV)

Demons are the power and influence behind idol worship.
They stirred him to jealousy with strange gods; with abominations they provoked him to anger. They sacrificed to demons that were no gods, to gods they had never known. Deuteronomy 32:16-17 (ESV)

No, I imply that what pagans sacrifice they offer to demons and not to God. 1 Corinthians 10:20 (ESV)

Continued⟶

Demons and Exorcism

Demons bring destruction into the lives of those they influence.
And when Jesus had stepped out of the boat, immediately there met him out of the tombs a man with an unclean spirit. He lived among the tombs. And no one could bind him anymore, not even with a chain, for he had often been bound with shackles and chains, but he wrenched the chains apart, and he broke the shackles in pieces. No one had the strength to subdue him. Night and day among the tombs and on the mountains he was always crying out and cutting himself with stones.
Mark 5:2-5 (ESV)

Demons were cast out of people by Jesus and his disciples.
But if it is by the Spirit of God that I cast out demons, then the kingdom of God has come upon you. Matthew 12:28 (ESV)

And proclaim as you go, saying, 'The kingdom of heaven is at hand.' Heal the sick, raise the dead, cleanse lepers, cast out demons.
Matthew 10:7-8 (ESV)

Then some of the itinerant Jewish exorcists undertook to invoke the name of the Lord Jesus over those who had evil spirits, saying, "I adjure you by the Jesus whom Paul proclaims." Seven sons of a Jewish high priest named Sceva were doing this. But the evil spirit answered them, "Jesus I know, and Paul I recognize, but who are you?" And the man in whom was the evil spirit leaped on them, mastered all of them and overpowered them, so that they fled out of that house naked and wounded. Acts 19:13-16 (ESV)

Demons were cast out of people by the name of Jesus.
The seventy-two returned with joy, saying, "Lord, even the demons are subject to us in your name!" Luke 10:17 (ESV)

Demons have less power than Christians and are not to be feared.
Behold, I have given you authority to tread on serpents and scorpions, and over all the power of the enemy, and nothing shall hurt you.
Luke 10:19 (ESV)

Denominationalism

A denomination is a subgroup within a larger group. There are literally thousands of Christian denominations in America today, representing hundreds of thousands of different churches. However, many wrongly assume that having different denominations means there is little doctrinal agreement among Christians. That is not the case. In fact, denominations were originally formed to preserve the unity among Christians. Allowing for disagreement over certain "non-essential" doctrinal issues, the very existence of denominations demonstrates that there is unity among Christians over "essential" doctrinal truths.

Historically, non-essential doctrine has been defined as any doctrine that does not bear directly on salvation. For example, some have wanted the freedom to celebrate communion or baptize in a certain way, believing that the Bible prescribed a particular form for these rituals, and denominations allow for differences in worship practice without disunity. Denominationalism allows for a distinction to be drawn between what is an important theological conviction (ex. mode of baptism), and what is a vital theological conviction (ex. deity of Jesus Christ). In other words, labeling some doctrine as "non-essential" is not the same as saying it is unimportant. The existence of denominations demonstrates that there are important differences of opinion, albeit on issues that are not vital.

We should picture denominations like different branches on a tree. Although each branch may look different, they all stem from a single trunk. In the case of denominations, the trunk from which all branches stem is the Apostles (Acts 2:42). Some of the essential doctrinal beliefs that all Christians denominations have historically embraced include: the deity of Jesus, the bodily death and resurrection of Jesus, the Trinity, and the return of Jesus.

The four main denominations of Christianity are Roman Catholicism, Eastern Orthodoxy, Anglicanism (Episcopalian) and Protestantism. Roman Catholicism is the oldest denomination, with each of the other denominations being formed as they broke away from Roman Catholicism. Within the Protestant denomination there are many other denominations such as: Methodist, Baptist, Congregational, Lutheran, Presbyterian, and Pentecostal. While each of these branches of the Christian faith have historically affirmed the essential doctrinal beliefs of the faith, some of these denominations have strayed from their theological roots in recent years.

Discerning God's Will

Discerning God's will requires understanding Jesus' teaching.
If anyone chooses to do God's will, he will find out whether my teaching comes from God or whether I speak on my own. John 7:17 (NIV)

Discerning God's will is possible because the Holy Spirit intercedes.
In the same way, the Spirit helps us in our weakness. We do not know what we ought to pray for, but the Spirit himself intercedes for us with groans that words cannot express. And he who searches our hearts knows the mind of the Spirit, because the Spirit intercedes for the saints in accordance with God's will. Romans 8:26-27 (NIV)

Discerning God's will comes as we renew our mind.
Do not conform any longer to the pattern of this world, but be transformed by the renewing of your mind. Then you will be able to test and approve what God's will is—his good, pleasing and perfect will. Romans 12:2 (NIV)

Discerning God's will means accepting the call to holiness.
It is God's will that you should be sanctified: that you should avoid sexual immorality... For God did not call us to be impure, but to live a holy life. Therefore, he who rejects this instruction does not reject man but God, who gives you his Holy Spirit. 1 Thessalonians 4:3, 7-8 (NIV)

Discerning God's will means embracing activities of faith.
Be joyful always; pray continually; give thanks in all circumstances, for this is God's will for you in Christ Jesus. 1 Thessalonians 5:16-18 (NIV)

Discerning God's will comes through wise counsel.
Plans fail for lack of counsel, but with many advisers they succeed. Proverbs 15:22 (NIV)

Discerning God's will means being filled with the Holy Spirit.
So then do not be foolish, but understand what the will of the Lord is. And do not get drunk with wine, for that is dissipation, but be filled with the Spirit, speaking to one another in psalms and hymns and spiritual songs, singing and making melody with your heart to the Lord; always giving thanks for all things in the name of our Lord Jesus Christ to God, even the Father; and be subject to one another in the fear of Christ. Ephesians 5:17-21 (NASB)

Discipleship

In discipleship our relationship with Jesus comes before all others.
Now great crowds accompanied him, and he turned and said to them, "If anyone comes to me and does not hate his own father and mother and wife and children and brothers and sisters, yes, and even his own life, he cannot be my disciple." Luke 14:24-26 (ESV)

In discipleship Jesus makes a relationship with us his priority.
While he was still speaking to the people, behold, his mother and his brothers stood outside, asking to speak to him. But he replied to the man who told him, "Who is my mother, and who are my brothers?" And stretching out his hand toward his disciples, he said, "Here are my mother and my brothers! For whoever does the will of my Father in heaven is my brother and sister and mother." Matthew 12:46-49 (ESV)

Discipleship results from Jesus choosing to reveal himself to us.
Then the disciples came and said to him, "Why do you speak to them in parables?" And he answered them, "To you it has been given to know the secrets of the kingdom of heaven, but to them it has not been given. Matthew 13:10-11 (ESV)

You did not choose me, but I chose you and appointed you that you should go and bear fruit and that your fruit should abide, so that whatever you ask the Father in my name, he may give it to you. John 15:16 (ESV)

Discipleship means receiving Jesus' commission to go.
And Jesus came and said to them, "All authority in heaven and on earth has been given to me. Go therefore and make disciples of all nations, baptizing them in the name of the Father and of the Son and of the Holy Spirit, teaching them to observe all that I have commanded you. And behold, I am with you always, to the end of the age." Matthew 28:18-20 (ESV)

Discipleship is confirmed in our lives by the love we show others.
By this all people will know that you are my disciples, if you have love for one another." John 13:35 (ESV)

Discipleship is confirmed as we bear fruit.
By this my Father is glorified, that you bear much fruit and so prove to be my disciples. John 15:8 (ESV)

Discipline within the Church

Discipline is the process of correcting the sinful attitudes or actions of others within the Church.

Discipline within the church is to follow a specific process.
"If your brother sins against you, go and show him his fault, just between the two of you. If he listens to you, you have won your brother over. But if he will not listen, take one or two others along, so that 'every matter may be established by the testimony of two or three witnesses.' If he refuses to listen to them, tell it to the church; and if he refuses to listen even to the church, treat him as you would a pagan or a tax collector. Matthew 18:15-17 (NIV)

Discipline within the church has the goal of teaching and salvation.
Some have rejected these and so have shipwrecked their faith. Among them are Hymenaeus and Alexander, whom I have handed over to Satan to be taught not to blaspheme. 1Timothy 1:18-20 (NIV)

It is actually reported that there is immorality among you, and immorality of such a kind as does not exist even among the Gentiles, that someone has his father's wife. You have become arrogant and have not mourned instead, so that the one who had done this deed would be removed from your midst. For I, on my part, though absent in body but present in spirit, have already judged him who has so committed this, as though I were present. In the name of our Lord Jesus, when you are assembled, and I with you in spirit, with the power of our Lord Jesus, I have decided to deliver such a one to Satan for the destruction of his flesh, so that his spirit may be saved in the day of the Lord Jesus. 1 Corinthians 5:1-5 (NASB)

Discipline in the church is needed as some reject sound doctrine.
Preach the word; be ready in season and out of season; reprove, rebuke, exhort, with great patience and instruction. For the time will come when they will not endure sound doctrine; but wanting to have their ears tickled, they will accumulate for themselves teachers in accordance to their own desires, and will turn away their ears from the truth and will turn aside to myths. But you, be sober in all things, endure hardship, do the work of an evangelist, fulfill your ministry. 2 Timothy 4:2-5 (NASB)

Continued ⟶

Discipline within the Church

Discipline within the church is to be done gently by the spiritual.
Brothers, if someone is caught in a sin, you who are spiritual should restore him gently. But watch yourself, or you also may be tempted. Carry each other's burdens, and in this way you will fulfill the law of Christ. Galatians 6:1-2 (NIV)

The Lord's bond-servant must not be quarrelsome, but be kind to all, able to teach, patient when wronged, with gentleness correcting those who are in opposition, if perhaps God may grant them repentance leading to the knowledge of the truth, and they may come to their senses and escape from the snare of the devil, having been held captive by him to do his will. 2 Timothy 2:24-26 (NASB)

Discipline within the church was practiced by early church leaders.
*But a man named Ananias, with his wife Sapphira, sold a piece of property, and kept back some of the price for himself, with his wife's full knowledge, and bringing a portion of it, he laid it at the apostles' feet. But Peter said, "Ananias, why has Satan filled your heart to lie to the Holy Spirit and to keep back some of the price of the land? While it remained unsold, did it not remain your own? And after it was sold, was it not under your control? Why is it that you have conceived this deed in your heart? You have not lied to men but to God." And as he heard these words, Ananias fell down and breathed his last; and great fear came over all who heard of it. The young men got up and covered him up, and after carrying him out, they buried him. Now there elapsed an interval of about three hours, and his wife came in, not knowing what had happened. And Peter responded to her, "Tell me whether you sold the land for such and such a price?" And she said, "Yes, that was the price." Then Peter said to her, "Why is it that you have agreed together to put the Spirit of the Lord to the test? Behold, the feet of those who have buried your husband are at the door, and they will carry you out as well." And immediately she fell at his feet and breathed her last, and the young men came in and found her dead, and they carried her out and buried her beside her husband. And great fear came over the whole church, and over all who heard of these things.
Acts 5:1-11 (NASB)*

Dispensationalism

Dispensationalism is a theological system that divides biblical history into seven successive periods (i.e. dispensations), and describes God as working with mankind differently in each period. Made popular by the writings of John Nelson Darby (1800-1882), dispensationalism is a relatively new theological system.

Fundamental to dispensationalism is the divide between the period of God's work in, through and for Israel, as the descendants of Abraham, and the period of God working in, through and for the Church, as those saved through faith in Jesus Christ. This divide is crucial as it influences the dispensational interpretation of God's work of salvation, as well as his work at the end of time, when Jesus Christ returns to set up his millennial kingdom. The dispensational view stands in contrast to historic "replacement" theology, which teaches that the church is fulfillment and receiver of the Old Testament promises to Israel. Dispensationalism teaches that God will finish a unique and separate work with Israel and the Church. The seven dispensations are:

The Dispensation of Innocence. The period beginning with creation, but before the fall of humanity into sin (Genesis 1-2).
The Dispensation of Conscience. The period beginning with the fall of humanity into sin and lasting until Noah's deliverance from the flood in the Ark (Genesis 3-9).
The Dispensation of Government. The period beginning with Noah and lasting until Abraham, as man began to establish himself on the earth (Genesis 10-11)
The Dispensation of Patriarchal Rule. The period beginning with Abraham and lasting until Moses, as God first called the Israelites to worship him (Genesis 12-Exodus 40).
The Dispensation of Mosaic Law. The period beginning with the Law given to Moses and lasting until the birth of Jesus Christ, including the writings of the Old Testament law, history, poetry and prophets.
The Dispensation of Grace. The period beginning with Christ's establishment of the new covenant through his death and the gathering of the Church to himself, as described in the four Gospels and the book of Acts.
The Dispensation of the Millennial Kingdom. The period beginning with Jesus Christ's return to rapture his Church and establish his 1000 year reign on the earth. This period has not started yet.

Divorce

Divorce law in the Old Testament protected women from the possibility of serial divorce.

If a man marries a woman who becomes displeasing to him because he finds something indecent about her, and he writes her a certificate of divorce, gives it to her and sends her from his house, and if after she leaves his house she becomes the wife of another man, and her second husband dislikes her and writes her a certificate of divorce, gives it to her and sends her from his house, or if he dies, then her first husband, who divorced her, is not allowed to marry her again after she has been defiled. That would be detestable in the eyes of the LORD.
Deuteronomy 24:1-4 (NIV)

Divorce was not a part of God's original design for marriage.

Some Pharisees came to him to test him. They asked, "Is it lawful for a man to divorce his wife for any and every reason?" "Haven't you read," he replied, "that at the beginning the Creator 'made them male and female,' and said, 'For this reason a man will leave his father and mother and be united to his wife, and the two will become one flesh'? So they are no longer two, but one. Therefore what God has joined together, let man not separate." Matthew 19:3-6 (NIV)

Divorce is a product of hardheartedness.

"Why then," they asked, "did Moses command that a man give his wife a certificate of divorce and send her away?" Jesus replied, "Moses permitted you to divorce your wives because your hearts were hard. But it was not this way from the beginning." Matthew 19:7-8 (NIV)

Divorce was explicitly prohibited by Paul, but in the event spouses do decide to divorce they are to remain unmarried or reconcile.

To the married I give this command (not I, but the Lord): A wife must not separate from her husband. But if she does, she must remain unmarried or else be reconciled to her husband. And a husband must not divorce his wife. 1 Corinthians 7:10-11 (NIV)

Elders

Elders were the leaders of the church in the New Testament. While there are three different words used interchangeably to describe their role, each word refers to different functions of the same office. The three terms are: elder (Greek *presbuteros*) which carries the sense of one who is older and wiser, overseer (Greek *episkopos*) which designates management responsibility, and pastor (Greek *poimen*) which means to shepherd.

Peter uses all three words in a single passage writing, "Therefore, I exhort the elders (*presbuteros*) among you...shepherd (*poimen*) the flock of God, exercising oversight (*episkos*)." (1 Peter 5:1 -2). These three terms together give us a picture of the role elders are to play in the local congregation. They are to wisely govern the church (*presbuteros*), exercising authority and managing ministry (*episkopos*), as well as caring for people spiritually (*poimen*).

Elders are the shepherds of God's flock, serving as examples.
Therefore, I exhort the elders among you, as your fellow elder and witness of the sufferings of Christ, and a partaker also of the glory that is to be revealed, shepherd the flock of God among you, exercising oversight not under compulsion, but voluntarily, according to the will of God; and not for sordid gain, but with eagerness; nor yet as lording it over those allotted to your charge, but proving to be examples to the flock. And when the Chief Shepherd appears, you will receive the unfading crown of glory. 1 Peter 5:1-4 (NASB)

Elders are to keep watch against those who would distort the truth.
"Be on guard for yourselves and for all the flock, among which the Holy Spirit has made you overseers, to shepherd the church of God which He purchased with His own blood. "I know that after my departure savage wolves will come in among you, not sparing the flock; and from among your own selves men will arise, speaking perverse things, to draw away the disciples after them. "Therefore be on the alert, remembering that night and day for a period of three years I did not cease to admonish each one with tears. Acts 20:28-31 (NASB)

Continued ⟶

Elders

Elders must have the desire and character for leadership.
The saying is trustworthy: If anyone aspires to the office of overseer, he desires a noble task. Therefore an overseer must be above reproach, the husband of one wife, sober-minded, self-controlled, respectable, hospitable, able to teach, not a drunkard, not violent but gentle, not quarrelsome, not a lover of money. He must manage his own household well, with all dignity keeping his children submissive, for if someone does not know how to manage his own household, how will he care for God's church? He must not be a recent convert, or he may become puffed up with conceit and fall into the condemnation of the devil. Moreover, he must be well thought of by outsiders, so that he may not fall into disgrace, into a snare of the devil.
1 Timothy 3:1-7 (ESV)

Elders were appointed in each congregation by Paul.
Paul and Barnabas appointed elders for them in each church and, with prayer and fasting, committed them to the Lord, in whom they had put their trust. Acts 14:23 (NIV)

Elders are to pray for the sick, anointing them with oil.
Is any one of you sick? He should call the elders of the church to pray over him and anoint him with oil in the name of the Lord.
James 5:14 (NIV)

Elders must be able to teach by example and endure opposition.
The Lord's bond-servant must not be quarrelsome, but be kind to all, able to teach, patient when wronged, with gentleness correcting those who are in opposition, if perhaps God may grant them repentance leading to the knowledge of the truth, and they may come to their senses and escape from the snare of the devil, having been held captive by him to do his will. 2 Timothy 2:24-26 (NASB)

Evangelism

The term "evangelism" comes from the Greek word *Evangelion*, from which we also get the word evangelical. Evangelicals are those who believe the Gospel is the "power of God for salvation" (Romans 1:16) and place a priority on proclaiming it publicly. In Mark 1:14 we read that Jesus went about "proclaiming the good news (*evangelion*) of God."

Evangelism begins with God, who lovingly calls us to repentance.
He prayed to the LORD and said, "Please LORD, was not this what I said while I was still in my own country? Therefore in order to forestall this I fled to Tarshish, for I knew that You are a gracious and compassionate God, slow to anger and abundant in lovingkindness, and one who relents concerning calamity. Jonah 4:2 (NASB)

But do not let this one fact escape your notice, beloved, that with the Lord one day is like a thousand years, and a thousand years like one day. The Lord is not slow about His promise, as some count slowness, but is patient toward you, not wishing for any to perish but for all to come to repentance. 2 Peter 3:8-9 (NASB)

Evangelism was at the heart of the command to make disciples.
Then Jesus came to them and said, "All authority in heaven and on earth has been given to me. Therefore go and make disciples of all nations, baptizing them in the name of the Father and of the Son and of the Holy Spirit, and teaching them to obey everything I have commanded you. And surely I am with you always, to the very end of the age." Matthew 28:18-20 (NIV)

Evangelism was at the heart of Jesus' mission and ministry.
*For the Son of Man came to seek and to save what was lost.
Luke 19:10 (NIV)*

Evangelism is an activity for which the world is waiting.
*"Do you not say, 'Four months more and then the harvest'? I tell you, open your eyes and look at the fields! They are ripe for harvest."
John 4: 35 (NIV)*

Continued——▶

Evangelism

Evangelism is a success only as God enables people to see the truth.
And even if our gospel is veiled, it is veiled to those who are perishing, in whose case the god of this world has blinded the minds of the unbelieving so that they might not see the light of the gospel of the glory of Christ, who is the image of God. For we do not preach ourselves but Christ Jesus as Lord, and ourselves as your bond-servants for Jesus' sake. For God, who said, "Light shall shine out of darkness," is the One who has shone in our hearts to give the Light of the knowledge of the glory of God in the face of Christ. 2 Corinthians 4:3-6 (NASB)

Evangelism brings a fuller understanding of our faith.
I pray that you may be active in sharing your faith, so that you will have a full understanding of every good thing we have in Christ. Philemon 1:6 (NIV)

Evangelism requires laborers for whom we are to pray.
After this the Lord appointed seventy-two others and sent them on ahead of him, two by two, into every town and place where he himself was about to go. And he said to them, "The harvest is plentiful, but the laborers are few. Therefore pray earnestly to the Lord of the harvest to send out laborers into his harvest. Go your way; behold, I am sending you out as lambs in the midst of wolves." Luke 10:1-3 (ESV)

Evangelism will continue until every nation and people hear.
And they sang a new song, saying, "Worthy are You to take the book and to break its seals; for You were slain, and purchased for God with Your blood men from every tribe and tongue and people and nation. Revelation 5:9 (NASB)

Evangelism and Sharing Your Faith

Sharing your faith with others is made easier if you have a relationship with the person with which you are sharing. However, having a relationship is not required. Many times in the New Testament the Apostles preached to crowds of people whom they did not know (Acts 2:14). However, the disciples never shared their faith without including Scripture in the discussion. Without a Scriptural (i.e. theological) basis for sharing our faith, we are left with sharing only our personal experience, which is often easily discounted as subjective.

Below is a question and answer based framework for sharing your faith that allows you to ask important questions and offer answers based upon Scriptural truth.

Have you heard the story of God's love for mankind?

It's a really simple and terrific story. God loves us, even though we are sinful, and sent his Son to die on a cross as a sin sacrifice.

> *"For God so loved the world that he gave his one and only Son, that whoever believes in him shall not perish but have eternal life. John 3:16 (NIV)*

> *But God demonstrates his own love for us in this: while we were still sinners, Christ died for us.*
> *Romans 5:8 (NIV)*

Have you ever thought of yourself as a sinner?

The Bible says that all have sinned and the wages of sin is death. By "wages," the Bible means that we earn deadly consequences from our sinful actions. Death includes both our emotional, physical and spiritual separation from our Creator, as well as any and all illness and certainly physical death.

> *For all have sinned and fall short of the glory of God.*
> *Romans 3:23 (NIV)*

> *For the wages of sin is death, but the gift of God is eternal life in Christ Jesus our Lord. Romans 6:23 (NIV)*

Continued ⟶

Evangelism and Sharing Your Faith

Have you seen the effects of death upon your life because of sin?

Even though sin brings death, God offers us life through faith in Jesus Christ. By believing that Jesus' death purchases our forgiveness, we are justified before God and have peace with God.

Therefore, since we have been justified through faith, we have peace with God through our Lord Jesus Christ, through whom we have gained access by faith into this grace in which we now stand. And we rejoice in the hope of the glory of God.
Romans 5:1-2 (NIV)

Do you know how to receive that eternal life?

The Bible says that all who call upon the name of the Lord will be saved. (Romans 10:13) Calling means confessing in prayer that we are sinful, asking God to forgive us our sinfulness and asking him for the power to follow after Jesus.

If we confess our sins, He is faithful and righteous to forgive us our sins and to cleanse us from all unrighteousness.
1 John 1:9 (NASB)

Would you let me lead you in prayer for salvation?

Heavenly Father,
We thank you for your love for us, which was demonstrated through the death of Jesus Christ. I recognize that I am a sinner and that my sin has brought death into my life. I thank you for the life offered through Jesus' resurrection, to all those who believe. I want to say that I believe, and ask that you would forgive my sin and that I would receive the eternal life promised through Jesus. Help me now to live a life that honors you. In Jesus' name I pray,
Amen.

Faith

Faith is being sure of what we hope for and certain of the unseen.
Now faith is the assurance of things hoped for, the conviction of things not seen. For by it the men of old gained approval. And without faith it is impossible to please Him, for he who comes to God must believe that He is and that He is a rewarder of those who seek Him.
Hebrews 11:1-2,6 (NASB)

The faith required by God is believing in Jesus as Savior.
Then they asked him, "What must we do to do the works God requires?" Jesus answered, "The work of God is this: to believe in the one he has sent." John 6: 28-29 (NIV)

Faith is essential for salvation.
Abram believed the Lord, and he credited it to him as righteousness. Genesis 15:6 (NIV)

For it is by grace you have been saved, through faith—and this not from yourselves, it is the gift of God—not by works, so that no one can boast. Ephesians 2:8-9 (NIV)

Faith was necessary for Jesus to do miracles.
He could not do any miracles there, except lay his hands on a few sick people and heal them. Mark 6:5 (NIV)

Faith in God can move mountains.
And Jesus answered them, "Have faith in God. Truly, I say to you, whoever says to this mountain, 'Be taken up and thrown into the sea,' and does not doubt in his heart, but believes that what he says will come to pass, it will be done for him. Therefore I tell you, whatever you ask in prayer, believe that you have received it, and it will be yours." Mark 11:22-24 (ESV)

Faith that saves is accompanied by works.
In the same way, faith by itself, if it is not accompanied by action, is dead. James 2:17 (NIV)

Fasting

Fasting is to go without food and/or drink, whether in part or in whole, in order to focus on prayer. In fasting we acknowledge that we have a need for God that is greater than even our need for food (Matthew 4:4). Every example of fasting in the Bible is joined with the activity of prayer. To fast without praying is simply to diet. While fasting does not compel God to act according to our prayers, it can help us be more receptive to hearing his voice and obeying his Word.

While we are certainly free to broaden our fasting to include abstinence from other activities (ex. watching television or shopping), and although these may be helpful in strengthening our discipline of prayer, the fasting mentioned in the Bible only includes abstaining from food.

Fasting was practiced by those seeking the Lord in prayer.
So I gave my attention to the Lord God to seek Him by prayer and supplications, with fasting, sackcloth and ashes. I prayed to the LORD my God and confessed and said, "Alas, O Lord, the great and awesome God, who keeps His covenant and lovingkindness for those who love Him and keep His commandments, we have sinned, committed iniquity, acted wickedly and rebelled, even turning aside from Your commandments and ordinances." Daniel 9:3-5 (NASB)

Fasting was practiced by Jesus in preparation for temptation.
Then Jesus was led up by the Spirit into the wilderness to be tempted by the devil. And after He had fasted forty days and forty nights, He then became hungry. And the tempter came and said to Him, "If You are the Son of God, command that these stones become bread." But He answered and said, "It is written, 'MAN SHALL NOT LIVE ON BREAD ALONE, BUT ON EVERY WORD THAT PROCEEDS OUT OF THE MOUTH OF GOD.'" Matthew 4:1-4 (NASB)

Fasting reminds us of the sustaining nature of obedience.
But he said to them, "I have food to eat that you know nothing about." Then his disciples said to each other, "Could someone have brought him food?" "My food," said Jesus, "is to do the will of him who sent me and to finish his work." John 4:32-34 (NIV)

Continued⟶

Fasting

Fasting was an indispensible part of early church worship.
While they were worshiping the Lord and fasting, the Holy Spirit said, "Set apart for me Barnabas and Saul for the work to which I have called them." So after they had fasted and prayed, they placed their hands on them and sent them off. Acts 13:2-3 (NIV)

Fasting is to be fueled by a longing for Jesus.
Now John's disciples and the Pharisees were fasting. Some people came and asked Jesus, "How is it that John's disciples and the disciples of the Pharisees are fasting, but yours are not?" Jesus answered, "How can the guests of the bridegroom fast while he is with them? They cannot, so long as they have him with them. But the time will come when the bridegroom will be taken from them, and on that day they will fast. Mark 2:18-20 (NIV)

Fasting in secret is rewarded by God who is invisible.
When you fast, do not look somber as the hypocrites do, for they disfigure their faces to show men they are fasting. I tell you the truth, they have received their reward in full. But when you fast, put oil on your head and wash your face, so that it will not be obvious to men that you are fasting, but only to your Father, who is unseen; and your Father, who sees what is done in secret, will reward you. Matthew 6:16-18 (NIV)

Fasting that God desires results in a compassion for the poor.
"Is this not the fast which I choose, to loosen the bonds of wickedness, to undo the bands of the yoke, and to let the oppressed go free and break every yoke? "Is it not to divide your bread with the hungry and bring the homeless poor into the house; when you see the naked, to cover him; and not to hide yourself from your own flesh? "Then your light will break out like the dawn, and your recovery will speedily spring forth; and your righteousness will go before you; the glory of the LORD will be your rear guard. "Then you will call, and the LORD will answer; you will cry, and He will say, 'Here I am.' If you remove the yoke from your midst, the pointing of the finger and speaking wickedness, and if you give yourself to the hungry and satisfy the desire of the afflicted, then your light will rise in darkness and your gloom will become like midday." Isaiah 58:6-10 (NASB)

Fear of Circumstances and God

Fear is possibly the most powerful human emotion, but not all fear is bad. God provides comfort in fearful circumstances for those who trust him, but there is wisdom in fearing God.

Fear of circumstances is overcome by Jesus Christ's peace.
Peace I leave with you; my peace I give to you. Not as the world gives do I give to you. Let not your hearts be troubled, neither let them be afraid. John 14:27 (ESV)

Fear of circumstances is not what God has given Christians.
For God gave us a spirit not of fear but of power and love and self-control. 2 Timothy 1:7 (ESV)

Fear of circumstances is conquered because the Lord is our help.
So we can confidently say, "The Lord is my helper; I will not fear; what can man do to me?" Hebrews 13:6 (ESV)

Fear of circumstances is cast out by the perfect love of God.
There is no fear in love, but perfect love casts out fear. For fear has to do with punishment, and whoever fears has not been perfected in love. 1 John 4:18 (ESV)

Fear of circumstances is overcome by God's comfort.
Even though I walk through the valley of the shadow of death, I will fear no evil, for you are with me; your rod and your staff, they comfort me. Psalm 23:4 (ESV)

Fear of God is appropriate and the beginning of true wisdom.
The fear of the LORD is the beginning of wisdom; all those who practice it have a good understanding. His praise endures forever! Psalm 111:10 (ESV)

The fear of the LORD is the beginning of knowledge; fools despise wisdom and instruction. Proverbs 1:7 (ESV)

Forgiving Others

Forgiving others is a part of our experiencing God's forgiveness.
For if you forgive men when they sin against you, your heavenly Father will also forgive you. But if you do not forgive men their sins, your Father will not forgive your sins. Matthew 6:14-15 (NIV)

Bear with each other and forgive whatever grievances you may have against one another. Forgive as the Lord forgave you.
Colossians 3:13 (NIV)

And when you stand praying, if you hold anything against anyone, forgive him, so that your Father in heaven may forgive you your sins. Mark 11:25 (NIV)

"But that slave went out and found one of his fellow slaves who owed him a hundred denarii; and he seized him and began to choke him, saying, 'Pay back what you owe.' "So his fellow slave fell to the ground and began to plead with him, saying, 'Have patience with me and I will repay you.' "But he was unwilling and went and threw him in prison until he should pay back what was owed. "So when his fellow slaves saw what had happened, they were deeply grieved and came and reported to their lord all that had happened. "Then summoning him, his lord said to him, 'You wicked slave, I forgave you all that debt because you pleaded with me. 'Should you not also have had mercy on your fellow slave, in the same way that I had mercy on you?' "And his lord, moved with anger, handed him over to the torturers until he should repay all that was owed him. "My heavenly Father will also do the same to you, if each of you does not forgive his brother from your heart." Matthew 18:28-35 (NASB)

Forgiving others is a reflection of God's mercy toward us.
For He Himself is kind to ungrateful and evil men. "Be merciful, just as your Father is merciful. Luke 6:35-36 (NASB)

Forgiving others is to be without end.
Then Peter came and said to Him, "Lord, how often shall my brother sin against me and I forgive him? Up to seven times?" Jesus said to him, "I do not say to you, up to seven times, but up to seventy times seven. Matthew 18:21-22 (NASB)

Freedom from Sin

Freedom from sin comes through faith in Jesus' resurrection.
Now if we have died with Christ, we believe that we shall also live with Him, knowing that Christ, having been raised from the dead, is never to die again; death no longer is master over Him. For the death that He died, He died to sin once for all; but the life that He lives, He lives to God. Even so consider yourselves to be dead to sin, but alive to God in Christ Jesus. Romans 6:8-11 (NASB)

Freedom from sin comes as we offer our body to righteousness.
Do not offer the parts of your body to sin, as instruments of wickedness, but rather offer yourselves to God, as those who have been brought from death to life; and offer the parts of your body to him as instruments of righteousness. Romans 6:12-13 (NIV)

Freedom from sin is a reality because we are under grace.
For sin shall not be your master, because you are not under law, but under grace. Romans 6:14 (NIV)

Freedom from sin allows us to offer ourselves to righteousness.
You have been set free from sin and have become slaves to righteousness. I put this in human terms because you are weak in your natural selves. Just as you used to offer the parts of your body in slavery to impurity and to ever-increasing wickedness, so now offer them in slavery to righteousness leading to holiness. Romans 6:18-19 (NIV)

Freedom from sin comes through his divine power.
Seeing that His divine power has granted to us everything pertaining to life and godliness, through the true knowledge of Him who called us by His own glory and excellence. For by these He has granted to us His precious and magnificent promises, so that by them you may become partakers of the divine nature, having escaped the corruption that is in the world by lust. 2 Peter 1:3-4 (NASB)

Freedom from sin gives us confidence that we can do all things.
I can do everything through him who gives me strength. Philippians 4:12-13 (NIV)

Continued——▶

Freedom from Sin

Freedom from sin comes as we crucify the sinful nature, carrying out the desires of the Spirit.

But I say, walk by the Spirit, and you will not carry out the desire of the flesh. For the flesh sets its desire against the Spirit, and the Spirit against the flesh; for these are in opposition to one another, so that you may not do the things that you please. But if you are led by the Spirit, you are not under the Law. Now the deeds of the flesh are evident, which are: immorality, impurity, sensuality, idolatry, sorcery, enmities, strife, jealousy, outbursts of anger, disputes, dissensions, factions, envying, drunkenness, carousing, and things like these, of which I forewarn you, just as I have forewarned you, that those who practice such things will not inherit the kingdom of God. But the fruit of the Spirit is love, joy, peace, patience, kindness, goodness, faithfulness, gentleness, self-control; against such things there is no law. Now those who belong to Christ Jesus have crucified the flesh with its passions and desires. If we live by the Spirit, let us also walk by the Spirit. Let us not become boastful, challenging one another, envying one another.
Galatians 5:16-26 (NASB)

Freedom from sin comes as we put to death the earthly nature.

Therefore consider the members of your earthly body as dead to immorality, impurity, passion, evil desire, and greed, which amounts to idolatry. For it is because of these things that the wrath of God will come upon the sons of disobedience, and in them you also once walked, when you were living in them. But now you also, put them all aside: anger, wrath, malice, slander, and abusive speech from your mouth. Do not lie to one another, since you laid aside the old self with its evil practices, and have put on the new self who is being renewed to a true knowledge according to the image of the One who created him--a renewal in which there is no distinction between Greek and Jew, circumcised and uncircumcised, barbarian, Scythian, slave and freeman, but Christ is all, and in all. So, as those who have been chosen of God, holy and beloved, put on a heart of compassion, kindness, humility, gentleness and patience; bearing with one another, and forgiving each other, whoever has a complaint against anyone; just as the Lord forgave you, so also should you. Beyond all these things put on love, which is the perfect bond of unity. Colossians 3:5-14 (NASB)

Gospel

The word Gospel means "good news" and comes from the Greek word *Evangelion,* from which we get the word evangelical. Evangelicals are those who believe the Gospel is the "power of God for salvation" (Romans 1:16) and place a priority on proclaiming it publicly. In Mark 1:14 we read that Jesus went about "proclaiming the good news *(evangelion)* of God."

First, the Gospel is a declaration of God's historic work to save his people, through the sacrificial death of Jesus, as a fulfillment of Old Testament prophecy. The Gospel isn't simply a New Testament message. The Gospel is an age old message, foretold by the Old Testament Law and Prophets. Paul alludes to the historic work of God when he writes that "...now a righteousness from God, apart from law, has been made known, to which the Law and the Prophets testify" (Romans 3:21). In fact, the Apostle Peter writes that Jesus was chosen for sacrifice from before the creation of the world. (1 Peter 1:20). And Jesus used the Old Testament to explain his ministry.

And beginning with Moses and all the Prophets, he explained to them what was said in all the Scriptures concerning himself. John 24:27 (NIV)

Second, the Gospel is also an affirmation that Jesus is both Savior and Lord, and the only way to the Father. Peter stood on the streets of Jerusalem and closed his message with this declaration , "Let all Israel be assured of this: God has made this Jesus, whom you crucified, both Lord and Christ" (Acts 2:36). Jesus said, "I'm the way, and the truth and the life, no one comes to the Father except through me" (John 14:6). The message of the Gospel is never presented as simply one option among many religions. The Gospel is presented in Scripture as the only one leading to life. The gospel is that "Salvation is found in no one else, for there is no other name under heaven given to men by which we must be saved" (Acts 4:12).

Finally, the Gospel is an invitation to confess and repent of one's sin (Romans 6:23), and to receive God's forgiveness and avoid his wrath (Romans 1:18). Essential to the Gospel is the doctrine of God's certain judgment and coming wrath because of mankind's sinfulness (Hebrews 4:13).

Continued→

Gospel

Without a thorough understanding of what we are being "saved" from, it is impossible to receive salvation itself. If the Gospel is simply a message of self-help or self-improvement, then Jesus didn't need to die. He only needed to teach and counsel and console, but he spilled his blood. He absorbed God's wrath against mankind, the punishment that was due each of us. Below is one of the most succinct explanations of the Gospel offered in Scripture.

*But now apart from the Law the righteousness of
God has been manifested, being witnessed by the Law
and the Prophets, even the righteousness of God
through faith in Jesus Christ for all those who believe;
for there is no distinction; for all have sinned and fall
short of the glory of God, being justified as a gift by
His grace through the redemption which is in Christ
Jesus; whom God displayed publicly as a propitiation
in His blood through faith This was to demonstrate
His righteousness, because in the forbearance of God
He passed over the sins previously committed; for
the demonstration, I say, of His righteousness at the
present time, so that He would be just and the justifier
of the one who has faith in Jesus.
Romans 3:21-26 (NASB)*

Gospel and Its Exclusivity and Inclusivity

The exclusivity of the Gospel is seen in the repeated claim that salvation is found only through faith in Jesus Christ.

The exclusivity of the Gospel was taught by Jesus.
Jesus answered, "I am the way and the truth and the life. No one comes to the Father except through me. John 14:6 (NIV)

The exclusivity of the Gospel was taught by the early church.
Salvation is found in no one else, for there is no other name under heaven given to men by which we must be saved." Acts 4:12 (NIV)

While the Gospel excludes all means of salvation, outside faith in Jesus, it does not put the burden of salvation upon anyone. Salvation is a gift given to all who believe in the sacrificial death and resurrection of Jesus Christ (Ephesians 2:8-9). In other words, no one who believes is excluded. In this respect the Gospel is far more inclusive than any other faith in the world, accepting everyone who believes regardless of race, gender or moral purity. While the means of salvation are exclusive, the Savior himself includes anyone who comes to him in faith. The inclusivity of the Gospel is a unique element of the Gospel's message.

The inclusivity of the Gospel was announced by Jesus.
"Come to Me, all who are weary and heavy-laden, and I will give you rest. Take My yoke upon you and learn from Me, for I am gentle and humble in heart, and YOU WILL FIND REST FOR YOUR SOULS. For My yoke is easy and My burden is light."
Matthew 11:28-30 (NASB)

The inclusivity of the Gospel was taught by the early church.
This righteousness from God comes through faith in Jesus Christ to all who believe. There is no difference, for all have sinned and fall short of the glory of God, and are justified freely by his grace through the redemption that came by Christ Jesus. Romans 3:22-24 (NIV)

Healing

Healing within the Bible included spiritual, psychological, physical and relational realities. Healing was a sign of Jesus' ministry as God's Savior (Luke 7:22-23), and healing was used by God to confirm the truth of the apostles preaching (Acts 14:3).

Healing comes to us through Jesus Christ's suffering on our behalf.
Surely our griefs He Himself bore, and our sorrows He carried; Yet we ourselves esteemed Him stricken, smitten of God, and afflicted. But He was pierced through for our transgressions, He was crushed for our iniquities; the chastening for our well-being fell upon Him, and by His scourging we are healed. Isaiah 53:4-5 (NASB)

For you have been called for this purpose, since Christ also suffered for you, leaving you an example for you to follow in His steps, WHO COMMITTED NO SIN, NOR WAS ANY DECEIT FOUND IN HIS MOUTH; and while being reviled, He did not revile in return; while suffering, He uttered no threats, but kept entrusting Himself to Him who judges righteously; and He Himself bore our sins in His body on the cross, so that we might die to sin and live to righteousness; for by His wounds you were healed. 1 Peter 2:21-24 (NASB)

Healing flowed through Jesus while he was on earth.
And wherever he went—into villages, towns or countryside—they placed the sick in the marketplaces. They begged him to let them touch even the edge of his cloak, and all who touched him were healed.
Mark 6:56 (NIV)

Healing power flowed to those who touched Jesus.
And all the people were trying to touch Him, for power was coming from Him and healing them all. Luke 6:19 (NASB)

Healing was a sign that Jesus is the Messiah.
And He answered and said to them, "Go and report to John what you have seen and heard: the BLIND RECEIVE SIGHT, the lame walk, the lepers are cleansed, and the deaf hear, the dead are raised up, the POOR HAVE THE GOSPEL PREACHED TO THEM. "Blessed is he who does not take offense at Me." Luke 7:22-23 (NASB)

Continued ⟶

Healing

Healing was a part of the ministry of the Apostles.
They went out and preached that men should repent. And they were casting out many demons and were anointing with oil many sick people and healing them. Mark 6:12-13 (NASB)

Healing from God flowed through Paul in extraordinary ways.
God was performing extraordinary miracles by the hands of Paul, so that handkerchiefs or aprons were even carried from his body to the sick, and the diseases left them and the evil spirits went out. Acts 19:11-12 (NASB)

Healing power from the Lord must be present to heal the sick.
One day as he was teaching, Pharisees and teachers of the law, who had come from every village of Galilee and from Judea and Jerusalem, were sitting there. And the power of the Lord was present for him to heal the sick. Luke 5:17 (NIV)

Healing prayer is a part of the ministry of the elders.
Is anyone among you sick? Then he must call for the elders of the church and they are to pray over him, anointing him with oil in the name of the Lord. James 5:14 (NASB)

Healing comes from God as we turn from sinfulness and seek him.
If my people, who are called by my name, will humble themselves and pray and seek my face and turn from their wicked ways, then will I hear from heaven and will forgive their sin and will heal their land. 2 Chronicles 7:14 (NIV)

Bless the LORD, O my soul, and all that is within me, bless His holy name. Bless the LORD, O my soul, and forget none of His benefits; who pardons all your iniquities, who heals all your diseases; who redeems your life from the pit, who crowns you with lovingkindness and compassion; Psalm 103:1-4 (NASB)

Hearing God's Voice

Hearing God's voice often comes over time and as others help us.
The LORD called Samuel a third time, and Samuel got up and went to Eli and said, "Here I am; you called me." Then Eli realized that the LORD was calling the boy. So Eli told Samuel, "Go and lie down, and if he calls you, say, 'Speak, LORD, for your servant is listening.' " So Samuel went and lay down in his place. 1 Samuel 3:8-9 (NIV)

Hearing God's voice often means listening for a gentle whisper.
So He said, "Go forth and stand on the mountain before the LORD " And behold, the LORD was passing by! And a great and strong wind was rending the mountains and breaking in pieces the rocks before the LORD; but the LORD was not in the wind. And after the wind an earthquake, but the LORD was not in the earthquake. After the earthquake a fire, but the LORD was not in the fire; and after the fire a sound of a gentle blowing. When Elijah heard it, he wrapped his face in his mantle and went out and stood in the entrance of the cave And behold, a voice came to him and said, "What are you doing here, Elijah?" 1 Kings 19:11-13 (NASB)

Hearing God's voice is an ability given to God's people.
His disciples asked him what this parable meant. He said, "The knowledge of the secrets of the kingdom of God has been given to you, but to others I speak in parables, so that, " 'though seeing, they may not see; though hearing, they may not understand.' Luke 8:9-10 (NIV)

Hearing God's voice is a means to following Jesus' lead.
The watchman opens the gate for him, and the sheep listen to his voice. He calls his own sheep by name and leads them out. When he has brought out all his own, he goes on ahead of them, and his sheep follow him because they know his voice. But they will never follow a stranger; in fact, they will run away from him because they do not recognize a stranger's voice." John 10:3-5 (NIV)

Heaven

Heaven is the place Jesus is preparing for those who believe in him.
"In My Father's house are many dwelling places; if it were not so, I would have told you; for I go to prepare a place for you. "If I go and prepare a place for you, I will come again and receive you to Myself, that where I am, there you may be also. "And you know the way where I am going." John 14:2-4 (NASB)

Now we know that if the earthly tent we live in is destroyed, we have a building from God, an eternal house in heaven, not built by human hands. Meanwhile we groan, longing to be clothed with our heavenly dwelling, because when we are clothed, we will not be found naked. 2 Corinthians 5:1-3 (NIV)

Heaven is where believers in Christ go immediately after death.
Jesus answered him, "I tell you the truth, today you will be with me in paradise." Luke 23:43 (NIV)

We are confident, I say, and would prefer to be away from the body and at home with the Lord. 2 Corinthians 5:8 (NIV)

Heaven, whether in part or in full, was seen by Paul.
I know a man in Christ who fourteen years ago--whether in the body I do not know, or out of the body I do not know, God knows--such a man was caught up to the third heaven. And I know how such a man-- whether in the body or apart from the body I do not know, God knows-- was caught up into Paradise and heard inexpressible words, which a man is not permitted to speak. 2 Corinthians 12:2-4 (NASB)

Heaven is the place of life eternal.
We always thank God, the Father of our Lord Jesus Christ, when we pray for you, since we heard of your faith in Christ Jesus and of the love that you have for all the saints, because of the hope laid up for you in heaven. Colossians 1:3-5 (ESV)

Hell

Hell is a place where God has the power to place us.
But I will warn you whom to fear: fear the One who, after He has killed, has authority to cast into hell; yes, I tell you, fear Him!
Luke 12:5 (NASB)

Hell is described as a place of torment.
"The time came when the beggar died and the angels carried him to Abraham's side. The rich man also died and was buried. In hell, where he was in torment, he looked up and saw Abraham far away, with Lazarus by his side. Luke 16:22-23 (NIV)

Hell was originally prepared for the devil and his angels.
"Then he will say to those on his left, 'Depart from me, you who are cursed, into the eternal fire prepared for the devil and his angels."
Matthew 25:41 (NIV)

Hell is where God is holding the rebellious angels.
For if God did not spare angels when they sinned, but cast them into hell and committed them to pits of darkness, reserved for judgment; and did not spare the ancient world, but preserved Noah, a preacher of righteousness, with seven others, when He brought a flood upon the world of the ungodly; and if He condemned the cities of Sodom and Gomorrah to destruction by reducing them to ashes, having made them an example to those who would live ungodly lives thereafter; and if He rescued righteous Lot, oppressed by the sensual conduct of unprincipled men (for by what he saw and heard that righteous man, while living among them, felt his righteous soul tormented day after day by their lawless deeds), then the Lord knows how to rescue the godly from temptation, and to keep the unrighteous under punishment for the day of judgment, and especially those who indulge the flesh in its corrupt desires and despise authority. Daring, self-willed, they do not tremble when they revile angelic majesties, whereas angels who are greater in might and power do not bring a reviling judgment against them before the Lord. 2 Peter 2:4-11 (NASB)

Hiddenness of God

The "hiddenness" of God is different than the blinding of minds by Satan (2 Corinthians 4:4), in that God has chosen to reveal himself to some while hiding himself from others.

The hiddenness of God is intentional on God's part.
And I know that this man was caught up into paradise—whether in the body or out of the body I do not know, God knows—and he heard things that cannot be told, which man may not utter.
1 Corinthians 12:3-4 (ESV)

The hiddenness of God is evident in some lacking understanding.
His disciples asked him what this parable meant. He said, "The knowledge of the secrets of the kingdom of God has been given to you, but to others I speak in parables, so that, " 'though seeing, they may not see; though hearing, they may not understand.' Luke 8:9-10 (NIV)

The hiddenness of God is evident in the condemnation of some.
Someone asked him, "Lord, are only a few people going to be saved?" He said to them, "Make every effort to enter through the narrow door, because many, I tell you, will try to enter and will not be able to. Once the owner of the house gets up and closes the door, you will stand outside knocking and pleading, 'Sir, open the door for us.' "But he will answer, 'I don't know you or where you come from.' "
Luke 13:23-25 (NIV)

The hiddenness of God is overcome as we diligently seek him.
"Ask and it will be given to you; seek and you will find; knock and the door will be opened to you. For everyone who asks receives; he who seeks finds; and to him who knocks, the door will be opened.
Matthew 7:7-8 (NIV)

Draw near to God and He will draw near to you. Cleanse your hands, you sinners; and purify your hearts, you double-minded. Be miserable and mourn and weep; let your laughter be turned into mourning and your joy to gloom. Humble yourselves in the presence of the Lord, and He will exalt you. James 4:8-10 (NASB)

The hiddenness of God is demonstrated in God opening minds.
Then he opened their minds to understand the Scriptures.
Luke 24:45 (ESV)

Holiness

Holiness, when used in relation to God, is not so much a singular attribute as it is a statement about his being. Holiness is the sum total of all of God's attributes, his moral purity, beauty, power, etc. Together these attributes make God holy, that is to say unique and unparalleled in nature, and thus separate from all other creatures in the universe by virtue of this combination of perfect attributes. In this sense, holiness necessarily implies a "separateness."

For Christians, the command to be holy is ultimately a command to live a unique and unparalleled life, a life increasingly marked by the attributes of God and thus separated from ungodliness.

Holiness is a description of God and is sung as his praise.
And the four living creatures, each one of them having six wings, are full of eyes around and within; and day and night they do not cease to say, "HOLY, HOLY, HOLY is THE LORD GOD, THE ALMIGHTY, WHO WAS AND WHO IS AND WHO IS TO COME."
Revelation 4:8 (NASB)

Holiness is the product of offering ourselves to righteousness.
I put this in human terms because you are weak in your natural selves. Just as you used to offer the parts of your body in slavery to impurity and to ever-increasing wickedness, so now offer them in slavery to righteousness leading to holiness. Romans 6:19 (NIV)

Holiness comes through Jesus Christ.
It is because of him that you are in Christ Jesus, who has become for us wisdom from God—that is, our righteousness, holiness and redemption. Therefore, as it is written: "Let him who boasts boast in the Lord."
1 Corinthians 1:30-31 (NIV)

Holiness is the call of God upon his people's lives.
As obedient children, do not conform to the evil desires you had when you lived in ignorance. But just as he who called you is holy, so be holy in all you do; for it is written: "Be holy, because I am holy."
1 Peter 1:14-16 (NIV)

Continued ——→

Holiness

Holiness is the result of thankfulness and reverence for God.

Since we have these promises, dear friends, let us purify ourselves from everything that contaminates body and spirit, perfecting holiness out of reverence for God. 2 Corinthians 7:1 (NIV)

Holiness is the reason we have been born again.

You were taught, with regard to your former way of life, to put off your old self, which is being corrupted by its deceitful desires; to be made new in the attitude of your minds; and to put on the new self, created to be like God in true righteousness and holiness.
Ephesians 4:22-24 (NIV)

Holiness is the product of God's grace teaching us.

For the grace of God that brings salvation has appeared to all men. It teaches us to say "No" to ungodliness and worldly passions, and to live self-controlled, upright and godly lives in this present age.
Titus 2:11-12 (NIV)

Holiness is the purpose of God's discipline in our lives.

Moreover, we have all had human fathers who disciplined us and we respected them for it. How much more should we submit to the Father of our spirits and live! Our fathers disciplined us for a little while as they thought best; but God disciplines us for our good, that we may share in his holiness. Hebrews 12:9-10 (NIV)

Holiness is the life prepared for judgment.

Since everything will be destroyed in this way, what kind of people ought you to be? You ought to live holy and godly lives as you look forward to the day of God and speed its coming. That day will bring about the destruction of the heavens by fire, and the elements will melt in the heat. 2 Peter 3:11-12 (NIV)

Holy Spirit

The Holy Spirit is God and a member of the Trinity.
Therefore go and make disciples of all nations, baptizing them in the name of the Father and of the Son and of the Holy Spirit.
Matthew 28:19 (NIV)

There are different kinds of gifts, but the same Spirit. There are different kinds of service, but the same Lord. There are different kinds of working, but the same God works all of them in all men.
1 Corinthians 12:4-6 (NIV)

There is one body and one Spirit—just as you were called to one hope when you were called—one Lord, one faith, one baptism; one God and Father of all, who is over all and through all and in all.
Ephesians 4:4-6 (NIV)

The Holy Spirit gives life to those who are in Christ.
You, however, are not in the flesh but in the Spirit, if in fact the Spirit of God dwells in you. Anyone who does not have the Spirit of Christ does not belong to him. But if Christ is in you, although the body is dead because of sin, the Spirit is life because of righteousness. If the Spirit of him who raised Jesus from the dead dwells in you, he who raised Christ Jesus from the dead will also give life to your mortal bodies through his Spirit who dwells in you. Romans 8:9-11 (ESV)

The Holy Spirit gives power, guidance, direction and gifts.
But you will receive power when the Holy Spirit comes on you; and you will be my witnesses." Acts 1:8 (NIV)

So I say, live by the Spirit, and you will not gratify the desires of the sinful nature. Galatians 5:16 (NIV)

Those who live according to the sinful nature have their minds set on what that nature desires; but those who live in accordance with the Spirit have their minds set on what the Spirit desires.
Romans 8:5 (NIV)

God also testifying with them, both by signs and wonders and by various miracles and by gifts of the Holy Spirit according to His own will.
Hebrews 2:4 (NASB)

Continued ⟶

Holy Spirit

The Holy Spirit physically dwells with Christians.

In Him, you also, after listening to the message of truth, the gospel of your salvation--having also believed, you were sealed in Him with the Holy Spirit of promise, who is given as a pledge of our inheritance, with a view to the redemption of God's own possession, to the praise of His glory. Ephesians 1:13-14 (NASB)

"He who believes in Me, as the Scripture said, 'From his innermost being will flow rivers of living water.'" But this He spoke of the Spirit, whom those who believed in Him were to receive; for the Spirit was not yet given, because Jesus was not yet glorified. John 7:38-39 (NASB)

Flee immorality. Every other sin that a man commits is outside the body, but the immoral man sins against his own body. Or do you not know that your body is a temple of the Holy Spirit who is in you, whom you have from God, and that you are not your own? 1 Corinthians 6:18-19 (NASB)

The Holy Spirit's presence in our lives guarantees our salvation.

In Him, you also, after listening to the message of truth, the gospel of your salvation--having also believed, you were sealed in Him with the Holy Spirit of promise, who is given as a pledge of our inheritance, with a view to the redemption of God's own possession, to the praise of His glory. Ephesians 1:13-14 (NASB)

Now He who prepared us for this very purpose is God, who gave to us the Spirit as a pledge. 2 Corinthians 5:5 (NASB)

The Holy Spirit produces the fruit of righteousness in our lives.

But the fruit of the Spirit is love, joy, peace, patience, kindness, goodness, faithfulness, gentleness, self-control; against such things there is no law. Galatians 5:22-23 (NASB)

The Holy Spirit is given as a helper who teaches us.

"But the Helper, the Holy Spirit, whom the Father will send in My name, He will teach you all things, and bring to your remembrance all that I said to you. John 14:26 (NASB)

Homosexuality

While homosexuality is only one of the many sins listed in the Bible, within our contemporary culture it is being presented by some as an alternative lifestyle. This makes homosexuality culturally unique, as few are presenting other sinful activities listed within the Bible (ex. drunkenness or adultery) as alternative ways to live.

Homosexuality was forbidden by the Old Testament law.
You shall not lie with a male as with a woman; it is an abomination. Leviticus 18:22 (ESV)

If a man lies with a male as with a woman, both of them have committed an abomination; they shall surely be put to death; their blood is upon them. Leviticus 20:13 (ESV)

Homosexuality is one of the many activities listed as contrary to God's law and thus sinful.
Now we know that the law is good, if one uses it lawfully, understanding this, that the law is not laid down for the just but for the lawless and disobedient, for the ungodly and sinners, for the unholy and profane, for those who strike their fathers and mothers, for murderers, the sexually immoral, men who practice homosexuality, enslavers, liars, perjurers, and whatever else is contrary to sound doctrine, in accordance with the gospel of the glory of the blessed God with which I have been entrusted. 1 Timothy 1:8-11 (ESV)

Homosexuality is unnatural, shameful and dishonorable to God.
For this reason God gave them up to dishonorable passions. For their women exchanged natural relations for those that are contrary to nature; and the men likewise gave up natural relations with women and were consumed with passion for one another, men committing shameless acts with men and receiving in themselves the due penalty for their error. Romans 1:26-27 (ESV)

Homosexuality is an unrighteous act and identified as one of the practices of those who will not inherit the kingdom of God.
Or do you not know that the unrighteous will not inherit the kingdom of God? Do not be deceived: neither the sexually immoral, nor idolaters, nor adulterers, nor men who practice homosexuality, nor thieves, nor the greedy, nor drunkards, nor revilers, nor swindlers will inherit the kingdom of God. 1 Corinthians 6:9-10 (ESV)

Jesus Christ

Jesus Christ is a both a name and a title. It is a combination of the first name of the man "Jesus," who was from Nazareth, and the ancient Greek title for "anointed" one, which is "Christ." In Hebrew, the title for "anointed" one is translated as "Messiah." To be the "anointed" one means to be the chosen one of God. Jesus is the Christ in that he was chosen by God to bear the sin of the world through his death.

Jesus Christ was recognized first by his disciples.

Now when Jesus came into the district of Caesarea Philippi, he asked his disciples, "Who do people say that the Son of Man is?" And they said, "Some say John the Baptist, others say Elijah, and others Jeremiah or one of the prophets." He said to them, "But who do you say that I am?" Simon Peter replied, "You are the Christ, the Son of the living God." And Jesus answered him, "Blessed are you, Simon Bar -Jonah! For flesh and blood has not revealed this to you, but my Father who is in heaven. Matthew 16:13-17 (ESV)

Jesus Christ was proclaimed as the means to forgiveness of sin.

Let all the house of Israel therefore know for certain that God has made him both Lord and Christ, this Jesus whom you crucified." Now when they heard this they were cut to the heart, and said to Peter and the rest of the apostles, "Brothers, what shall we do?" And Peter said to them, "Repent and be baptized every one of you in the name of Jesus Christ for the forgiveness of your sins, and you will receive the gift of the Holy Spirit. For the promise is for you and for your children and for all who are far off, everyone whom the Lord our God calls to himself." Acts 2:36-39 (ESV)

Jesus Christ provides righteousness to all who believe in him.

But now a righteousness from God, apart from law, has been made known, to which the Law and the Prophets testify. This righteousness from God comes through faith in Jesus Christ to all who believe. Romans 3:21-22 (NIV)

Jesus Christ's Deity

Jesus Christ's deity is seen in being with God in the beginning.
In the beginning was the Word, and the Word was with God, and the Word was God. He was with God in the beginning. The Word became flesh and made his dwelling among us. We have seen his glory, the glory of the One and Only, who came from the Father, full of grace and truth. John 1:1-2, 14 (NIV)

Jesus Christ's deity is evident in his creative role.
Through him all things were made; without him nothing was made that has been made. John 1:3 (NIV)

Jesus Christ's deity is affirmed in his sustaining role in creation.
In him was life, and that life was the light of men. John 1:4 (NIV)

Jesus Christ's deity was clearly declared by Paul.
Theirs are the patriarchs, and from them is traced the human ancestry of Christ, who is God over all, forever praised! Amen. Romans 9:5 (NIV)

Jesus Christ's deity means that he physically represents God.
He is the image of the invisible God, the firstborn of all creation. For by him all things were created, in heaven and on earth, visible and invisible, whether thrones or dominions or rulers or authorities—all things were created through him and for him. And he is before all things, and in him all things hold together. And he is the head of the body, the church. He is the beginning, the firstborn from the dead, that in everything he might be preeminent. For in him all the fullness of God was pleased to dwell, and through him to reconcile to himself all things, whether on earth or in heaven, making peace by the blood of his cross. Colossians 1:15-20 (NIV)

Jesus Christ's deity means that God's fullness dwells in Jesus.
For in Him all the fullness of Deity dwells in bodily form. Colossians 2:9 (NASB)

Jesus Christ's deity is affirmed in his role as a mediator.
For there is one God, and one mediator also between God and men, the man Christ Jesus. 1 Timothy 2:5 (NASB)

67

Jesus Christ's Resurrection

Jesus Christ's resurrection was foretold in the Old Testament.
"As for me, I know that my Redeemer lives, and at the last He will take His stand on the earth. "Even after my skin is destroyed, yet from my flesh I shall see God; whom I myself shall behold, and whom my eyes will see and not another. My heart faints within me!
Job 19:25-27 (NASB)

"Now at that time Michael, the great prince who stands guard over the sons of your people, will arise And there will be a time of distress such as never occurred since there was a nation until that time; and at that time your people, everyone who is found written in the book, will be rescued. "Many of those who sleep in the dust of the ground will awake, these to everlasting life, but the others to disgrace and everlasting contempt. "Those who have insight will shine brightly like the brightness of the expanse of heaven, and those who lead the many to righteousness, like the stars forever and ever. Daniel 12:1-3 (NASB)

Jesus Christ's resurrection was predicted by Jesus.
From that time Jesus began to show his disciples that he must go to Jerusalem and suffer many things from the elders and chief priests and scribes, and be killed, and on the third day be raised.
Matthew 16:21 (ESV)

Jesus Christ's resurrection prediction was understood by his enemies and they took precautions against the body being stolen.
The next day, that is, after the day of Preparation, the chief priests and the Pharisees gathered before Pilate and said, "Sir, we remember how that impostor said, while he was still alive, 'After three days I will rise.' Therefore order the tomb to be made secure until the third day, lest his disciples go and steal him away and tell the people, 'He has risen from the dead,' and the last fraud will be worse than the first." Pilate said to them, "You have a guard of soldiers. Go, make it as secure as you can." So they went and made the tomb secure by sealing the stone and setting a guard. Matthew 27:62-66 (ESV)

Jesus Christ's resurrection was attested to by the apostles.
And with great power the apostles were giving their testimony to the resurrection of the Lord Jesus, and great grace was upon them all.
Acts 4:33 (ESV)

Continued ⟶

68

Jesus Christ's Resurrection

Jesus Christ's resurrection was seen by angels, men and women.
And they found the stone rolled away from the tomb, but when they went in they did not find the body of the Lord Jesus. While they were perplexed about this, behold, two men stood by them in dazzling apparel. And as they were frightened and bowed their faces to the ground, the men said to them, "Why do you seek the living among the dead? He is not here, but has risen. Remember how he told you, while he was still in Galilee, that the Son of Man must be delivered into the hands of sinful men and be crucified and on the third day rise." Luke 24:2-7 (ESV)

When he was at table with them, he took the bread and blessed and broke it and gave it to them. And their eyes were opened, and they recognized him. And he vanished from their sight. Luke 24:30-31 (ESV)

Then he said to Thomas, "Put your finger here, and see my hands; and put out your hand, and place it in my side. Do not disbelieve, but believe." Thomas answered him, "My Lord and my God!" Jesus said to him, "Have you believed because you have seen me? Blessed are those who have not seen and yet have believed." John 20:26-29 (ESV)

Afterward he appeared to the eleven themselves as they were reclining at table, and he rebuked them for their unbelief and hardness of heart, because they had not believed those who saw him after he had risen. Mark 16:14 (ESV)

Then he appeared to more than five hundred brothers at one time, most of whom are still alive, though some have fallen asleep. Then he appeared to James, then to all the apostles. Last of all, as to one untimely born, he appeared also to me. 1 Corinthians 15:6-8 (ESV)

Jesus Christ's resurrection will be shared in by all Christians.
For if we have been united with him in a death like his, we shall certainly be united with him in a resurrection like his. Romans 6:5 (ESV)

Blessed be the God and Father of our Lord Jesus Christ! According to his great mercy, he has caused us to be born again to a living hope through the resurrection of Jesus Christ from the dead, to an inheritance that is imperishable, undefiled, and unfading, kept in heaven for you. 1 Peter 1:3-4 (ESV)

Jesus Christ's Return

Jesus Christ's return will be surprising.
So you also must be ready, because the Son of Man will come at an hour when you do not expect him. Matthew 24:44 (NIV)

Jesus Christ's return will be bodily and visible.
"Men of Galilee," they said, "why do you stand here looking into the sky? This same Jesus, who has been taken from you into heaven, will come back in the same way you have seen him go into heaven."
Acts 1:11 (NIV)

Jesus Christ's return will be personal.
For the Lord himself will come down from heaven, with a loud command, with the voice of the archangel and with the trumpet call of God, and the dead in Christ will rise first. After that, we who are still alive and are left will be caught up together with them in the clouds to meet the Lord in the air. And so we will be with the Lord forever. Therefore encourage each other with these words. 1 Thessalonians 4:16-18 (NIV)

Jesus Christ's return will bring salvation to those waiting for him.
Christ was sacrificed once to take away the sins of many people; and he will appear a second time, not to bear sin, but to bring salvation to those who are waiting for him. Hebrews 9:28 (NIV)

Jesus Christ's return will be soon and we are to be patient.
Be patient, then, brothers, until the Lord's coming. See how the farmer waits for the land to yield its valuable crop and how patient he is for the autumn and spring rains. You too, be patient and stand firm, because the Lord's coming is near. James 5:7-8 (NIV)

Jesus Christ's return is something for which we should be eager.
He who testifies to these things says, "Yes, I am coming soon." Amen. Come, Lord Jesus. Revelation 22:20 (NIV)

Jesus Christ's return will bring judgment.
It was also about these men that Enoch, in the seventh generation from Adam, prophesied, saying, "Behold, the Lord came with many thousands of His holy ones, to execute judgment upon all, and to convict all the ungodly of all their ungodly deeds which they have done in an ungodly way, and of all the harsh things which ungodly sinners have spoken against Him." Jude 14-15 (NASB)

Judgment by God

The judgment by God will come to all people.
Nothing in all creation is hidden from God's sight. Everything is uncovered and laid bare before the eyes of him to whom we must give account. Hebrews 4:13 (NIV)

The judgment by God will come to Christians for their works, and will bring reward and loss.
If any man builds on this foundation using gold, silver, costly stones, wood, hay or straw, his work will be shown for what it is, because the Day will bring it to light. It will be revealed with fire, and the fire will test the quality of each man's work. If what he has built survives, he will receive his reward. If it is burned up, he will suffer loss; he himself will be saved, but only as one escaping through the flames. 1 Corinthians 3:12-15 (NIV)

The judgment by God will condemn all not in the book of life.
Then another book was opened, which is the book of life. And the dead were judged by what was written in the books, according to what they had done. And the sea gave up the dead who were in it, Death and Hades gave up the dead who were in them, and they were judged, each one of them, according to what they had done. Then Death and Hades were thrown into the lake of fire. This is the second death, the lake of fire. And if anyone's name was not found written in the book of life, he was thrown into the lake of fire. Revelation 20:12-15 (NIV)

The judgment by God will includes saints judging the world and angels.
Do you not know that the saints will judge the world? And if you are to judge the world, are you not competent to judge trivial cases? Do you not know that we will judge angels? How much more the things of this life! 1 Corinthians 6:2-3 (NIV)

The judgment by God results in some going to Hell.
"Then they themselves also will answer, 'Lord, when did we see You hungry, or thirsty, or a stranger, or naked, or sick, or in prison, and did not take care of You?' "Then He will answer them, 'Truly I say to you, to the extent that you did not do it to one of the least of these, you did not do it to Me.' "These will go away into eternal punishment, but the righteous into eternal life." Matthew 25:44-46 (NASB)

Judgment of Others

We should never pass judgment on other's motives, and judgment of others' actions should only be based upon Scripture. We should only pass judgment after first admitting our own sinfulness, and only when recognizing that our judgments may be clouded by sin. Even our clearest and most sane judgments can be infected with sin, so we must offer our judgments humbly.

Judgment of others will be the measure by which we are judged.
"Do not judge so that you will not be judged. "For in the way you judge, you will be judged; and by your standard of measure, it will be measured to you. Matthew 7:1-2 (NASB)

Judgment of others is to be humbly offered, recognizing our sin.
"Why do you look at the speck of sawdust in your brother's eye and pay no attention to the plank in your own eye? How can you say to your brother, 'Let me take the speck out of your eye,' when all the time there is a plank in your own eye? You hypocrite, first take the plank out of your own eye, and then you will see clearly to remove the speck from your brother's eye. Matthew 7:3-5 (NIV)

Judgment of others is expected, when based on Scripture.
For I, on my part, though absent in body but present in spirit, have already judged him who has so committed this, as though I were present. In the name of our Lord Jesus, when you are assembled, and I with you in spirit, with the power of our Lord Jesus, I have decided to deliver such a one to Satan for the destruction of his flesh, so that his spirit may be saved in the day of the Lord Jesus.
1 Corinthians 5:3-5 (NASB)

For what have I to do with judging outsiders? Do you not judge those who are within the church? But those who are outside, God judges. REMOVE THE WICKED MAN FROM AMONG YOURSELVES.
1 Corinthians 5:12-13 (NASB)

Judgment of a prophet's words is expected from others.
Let two or three prophets speak, and let the others pass judgment.
1 Corinthians 14:29 (NIV)

Law

The Law was first given by God to Moses, while he was with God on Mount Sinai (Exodus 19-20). The Law of the Old Testament is a revelation of God's perfect character (Psalm 19:7), and keeping the Law was a part of the old covenant (agreement) God made with Israel. For the Israelites to maintain their covenant relationship with God, they had to keep all of the Law, which included civil law (national government) ceremonial law (feasts and sacrifices for worship), and moral law (Ten Commandments).

Ultimately, the requirements of the Law were completely and perfectly fulfilled only by Jesus Christ (Romans 8:3-4; Hebrews 4:15). This means God's character, as described in the Law of the Old Testament, has been fully revealed in Jesus Christ. In fact, the requirements of the Law are meant to help us see our need for the forgiveness provided through Jesus Christ's death (Galatians 3:24-25), and those who trust in Jesus Christ's death on the cross come under the new covenant of grace, which is outline in the New Testament (Romans 3:21-24).

This does not mean that the Old Testament, which describes the old covenant, should not be read. It simply means that the Old Testament will only fully be understood in light of the New Testament. Jesus himself said, "not the least stroke of a pen, will by any means disappear from the Law until everything is accomplished" (Matthew 5:18). Ultimately, our understanding the Old Testament Law will help us understand the significance of Jesus Christ's moral perfection and sacrificial death on our behalf. While it's true that many of the ceremonial and sacrificial laws are no longer applicable to those under the new covenant, these laws continue to help us understand the righteous character God expects his people to possess (Acts 15:1-35).

Paul affirms the Law as well, writing "the law is holy, and the commandment is holy, righteous and good" (Romans 7:12). Therefore the responsibility of those living under the new covenant of grace is to: identify that part of God's character revealed in a particular law, celebrate Jesus Christ's fulfillment of that law on our behalf, and then figure out how to best emulate the character of God described in the Law in an effort to follow after Jesus Christ in life.

Marriage

Marriage was instituted by God at creation.
For this reason a man will leave his father and mother and be united to his wife, and they will become one flesh. Genesis 2:24 (NIV)

Marriage is a picture of God's love for his people.
Then the LORD said to me, "Go again, love a woman who is loved by her husband, yet an adulteress, even as the LORD loves the sons of Israel, though they turn to other gods and love raisin cakes."
Hosea 3:1 (NASB)

Marriage was affirmed by Jesus as a lifelong, heterosexual union.
He answered, "Have you not read that he who created them from the beginning made them male and female, and said, 'Therefore a man shall leave his father and his mother and hold fast to his wife, and the two shall become one flesh'? So they are no longer two but one flesh. What therefore God has joined together, let not man separate."
Matthew 19:4-6 (ESV)

Marriage is to provide mutual care for spouses.
Nevertheless, each individual among you also is to love his own wife even as himself, and the wife must see to it that she respects her husband. Ephesians 5:33 (NASB)

Marriage of believers is to be only with other believers.
Do not be yoked together with unbelievers. For what do righteousness and wickedness have in common? Or what fellowship can light have with darkness? 2 Corinthians 6:14 (NIV)

Marriage is a picture of Christ's union with the Church.
"For this reason a man will leave his father and mother and be united to his wife, and the two will become one flesh." This is a profound mystery—but I am talking about Christ and the church.
Ephesians 5:31-32 (NIV)

Marriage is a help for those struggling with immorality.
But since there is so much immorality, each man should have his own wife, and each woman her own husband. The husband should fulfill his marital duty to his wife, and likewise the wife to her husband.
1 Corinthians 7:2-3 (NIV)

Miracles

The Bible is full of reports of miracles. There are reports of a talking serpent (Genesis 3:1) and donkey (Numbers 22:28), as well as a large sea creature that carries Jonah in his stomach for three days, only to spit him up on a beach (Jonah 1:17; 2:10), and numerous healings. And of course, there is the greatest miracle of all, Jesus Christ being raised from the grave after three days (John 2:22; 21:14). To believe the Bible requires believing in miracles.

Miracles brought deliverance for the Jews.
"So I will stretch out My hand and strike Egypt with all My miracles which I shall do in the midst of it; and after that he will let you go.
Exodus 3:20 (NASB)

Miracles were offered as evidence of Jesus Christ's deity.
Believe me when I say that I am in the Father and the Father is in me; or at least believe on the evidence of the miracles themselves.
John 14:11 (NIV)

Miracle working was an expectation of Jesus for his disciples.
I tell you the truth, anyone who has faith in me will do what I have been doing. He will do even greater things than these, because I am going to the Father. And I will do whatever you ask in my name, so that the Son may bring glory to the Father. You may ask me for anything in my name, and I will do it. John 14:12-14 (NIV)

Miracles from God were extraordinary through Paul in Ephesus.
God did extraordinary miracles through Paul, so that even handkerchiefs and aprons that had touched him were taken to the sick, and their illnesses were cured and the evil spirits left them.
Acts 19:11-12 (NIV)

Miracle working is a gift given to some within the Church by the Holy Spirit.
Now you are the body of Christ, and each one of you is a part of it. And in the church God has appointed first of all apostles, second prophets, third teachers, then workers of miracles, also those having gifts of healing, those able to help others, those with gifts of administration, and those speaking in different kinds of tongues.
1 Corinthians 12:27-28 (NIV)

Money

Money handled wisely is a means for storing up treasure in heaven.
"Do not store up for yourselves treasures on earth, where moth and rust destroy, and where thieves break in and steal. "But store up for yourselves treasures in heaven, where neither moth nor rust destroys, and where thieves do not break in or steal; for where your treasure is, there your heart will be also. "No one can serve two masters; for either he will hate the one and love the other, or he will be devoted to one and despise the other You cannot serve God and wealth.
Matthew 6:19-21, 24 (NASB)

Money can make it difficult for a rich person to get into heaven.
And Jesus said to his disciples, "Truly, I say to you, only with difficulty will a rich person enter the kingdom of heaven. Again I tell you, it is easier for a camel to go through the eye of a needle than for a rich person to enter the kingdom of God." When the disciples heard this, they were greatly astonished, saying, "Who then can be saved?" But Jesus looked at them and said, "With man this is impossible, but with God all things are possible." Matthew 19:23-26 (ESV)

Money is an opportunity to give, even out of our poverty.
And He sat down opposite the treasury, and began observing how the people were putting money into the treasury; and many rich people were putting in large sums. A poor widow came and put in two small copper coins, which amount to a cent. Calling His disciples to Him, He said to them, "Truly I say to you, this poor widow put in more than all the contributors to the treasury; for they all put in out of their surplus, but she, out of her poverty, put in all she owned, all she had to live on." Mark 12:41-44 (NASB)

Money can choke out the seed of God's Word in our lives.
"The seed which fell among the thorns, these are the ones who have heard, and as they go on their way they are choked with worries and riches and pleasures of this life, and bring no fruit to maturity. "But the seed in the good soil, these are the ones who have heard the word in an honest and good heart, and hold it fast, and bear fruit with perseverance. Luke 8:14-15 (NASB)

Continued⟶

Money

Money is a means for testing the sincerity of our faith.
But just as you excel in everything—in faith, in speech, in knowledge, in complete earnestness and in your love for us—see that you also excel in this grace of giving. I am not commanding you, but I want to test the sincerity of your love by comparing it with the earnestness of others. For you know the grace of our Lord Jesus Christ, that though he was rich, yet for your sakes he became poor, so that you through his poverty might become rich. 2 Corinthians 8:7-9 (NIV)

Money can lead us into temptation and destroy our faith.
But those who desire to be rich fall into temptation, into a snare, into many senseless and harmful desires that plunge people into ruin and destruction. For the love of money is a root of all kinds of evils. It is through this craving that some have wandered away from the faith and pierced themselves with many pangs. 1 Timothy 6:9-10 (ESV)

Money is an opportunity to be generous and rich in good deeds.
Command those who are rich in this present world not to be arrogant nor to put their hope in wealth, which is so uncertain, but to put their hope in God, who richly provides us with everything for our enjoyment. Command them to do good, to be rich in good deeds, and to be generous and willing to share. In this way they will lay up treasure for themselves as a firm foundation for the coming age, so that they may take hold of the life that is truly life. 1 Timothy 6:17-19 (NIV)

Money is to be given by God's people generously and cheerfully.
The point is this: whoever sows sparingly will also reap sparingly, and whoever sows bountifully will also reap bountifully. Each one must give as he has decided in his heart, not reluctantly or under compulsion, for God loves a cheerful giver. And God is able to make all grace abound to you, so that having all sufficiency in all things at all times, you may abound in every good work. 2 Corinthians 9:6-8 (ESV)

Continued——▶

Money

Money is to be given to support the ministries of the local church.
Who serves as a soldier at his own expense? Who plants a vineyard without eating any of its fruit? Or who tends a flock without getting some of the milk? Do I say these things on human authority? Does not the Law say the same? For it is written in the Law of Moses, "You shall not muzzle an ox when it treads out the grain." Is it for oxen that God is concerned? Does he not speak entirely for our sake? It was written for our sake, because the plowman should plow in hope and the thresher thresh in hope of sharing in the crop. If we have sown spiritual things among you, is it too much if we reap material things from you? If others share this rightful claim on you, do not we even more?
1 Corinthians 9:7-12 (ESV)

Anyone who receives instruction in the word must share all good things with his instructor. Galatians 6:6 (ESV)

Money is to be given to the church regularly and proportionally.
On the first day of every week, each one of you should set aside a sum of money in keeping with his income, saving it up, so that when I come no collections will have to be made. 1 Corinthians 16:2 (ESV)

Money handled wisely can provide an assurance of salvation.
And Zacchaeus stood and said to the Lord, "Behold, Lord, the half of my goods I give to the poor. And if I have defrauded anyone of anything, I restore it fourfold." And Jesus said to him, "Today salvation has come to this house, since he also is a son of Abraham. For the Son of Man came to seek and to save the lost." Luke 19:8-10 (ESV)

Names of God

The names of God are titles that capture his character, as well as his purposes for his people The list below is not exhaustive.

El Shaddai. God almighty or all sufficient (Genesis 17:1).

Adonai. Rendered as "Lord" in English Bibles, is always used in the plural form and means master (Exodus 4:10).

Jehovah or Yahweh. Rendered "LORD" in English Bibles, although in older translations it may appear as Jehovah. This is the personal name of God, first revealed to Moses on Mt. Sinai (Exodus 3:14), and is form of the verb meaning "to be." The spelling of the name is a transliteration of four consonant letters in the Hebrew language, YHWH.

Jehovah-Jireh. "The Lord will provide" (Genesis 22:14). This denotes God providing what is needed for life.

Jehovah-Rophe. "The Lord heals" (Exodus 15:22-26). This denotes God's care of us spiritually, emotionally and physically.

Jehovah-Nissi. "The Lord is Our Banner" (Exodus 17:15). This denotes God's protection and deliverance for his people.

Jehovah-M'Kaddesh. "The Lord Sanctifies" (Leviticus 20:7-8). This denotes God's work to set apart his people for lives of holiness.

Jehovah-Shalom. "The Lord Our Peace" (Judges 6:24). Denotes God's completed work to provide peace with him, oneself and others.

Jehovah-Tsidkenu. "The Lord Our Righteousness" (Jeremiah 23:6). Denotes God's provision of righteousness for the unrighteous.

Jehovah-Rohi. "The Lord Our Shepherd" (Psalm 23:1). Denotes God's work to guide and care for his people.

Jehovah-Shammah. "The Lord is There" (Ezek. 48:35). Denotes God's presence will be with his people.

Obedience

Obedience to Jesus is an indication of our love for Jesus.
Whoever has my commands and obeys them, he is the one who loves me. He who loves me will be loved by my Father, and I too will love him and show myself to him." John 14:21 (NIV)

Jesus replied, "If anyone loves me, he will obey my teaching. My Father will love him, and we will come to him and make our home with him. He who does not love me will not obey my teaching. These words you hear are not my own; they belong to the Father who sent me.
John 14:23-24 (NIV)

Obedience to Jesus provides assurance we will remain in his love.
If you obey my commands, you will remain in my love, just as I have obeyed my Father's commands and remain in his love.
John 15:10 (NIV)

Obedience to Jesus' commands means loving one another.
And this is love: that we walk in obedience to his commands. As you have heard from the beginning, his command is that you walk in love.
2 John 1:6 (NIV)

Obedience is required in order to escape punishment.
He will punish those who do not know God and do not obey the gospel of our Lord Jesus. They will be punished with everlasting destruction and shut out from the presence of the Lord and from the majesty of his power. 2 Thessalonians 1:8-9 (NIV)

Obedience to Scripture is a requirement for fellowship.
As for you, brothers, do not grow weary in doing good. If anyone does not obey what we say in this letter, take note of that person, and have nothing to do with him, that he may be ashamed. Do not regard him as an enemy, but warn him as a brother.
2 Thessalonians 3:13-15 (ESV)

Prayer

Prayer was and is an activity of Jesus.
"Simon, Simon, behold, Satan demanded to have you, that he might sift you like wheat, but I have prayed for you that your faith may not fail. And when you have turned again, strengthen your brothers."
Luke 22:31-32 (ESV)

But now even more the report about him went abroad, and great crowds gathered to hear him and to be healed of their infirmities. But he would withdraw to desolate places and pray. Luke 5:15-16 (ESV)

Consequently, he is able to save to the uttermost those who draw near to God through him, since he always lives to make intercession for them. Hebrews 7:25 (ESV)

Prayer is an activity of the Holy Spirit.
Likewise the Spirit helps us in our weakness. For we do not know what to pray for as we ought, but the Spirit himself intercedes for us with groanings too deep for words. Romans 8:26 (ESV)

Prayer is a means to experiencing God's healing.
If my people, who are called by my name, will humble themselves and pray and seek my face and turn from their wicked ways, then will I hear from heaven and will forgive their sin and will heal their land.
2 Chronicles 7:14 (NIV)

Prayer is to be offered in Jesus Christ's name and for his glory.
And I will do whatever you ask in my name, so that the Son may bring glory to the Father. You may ask me for anything in my name, and I will do it. John 14:13-14 (NIV)

Prayer is made effective through agreement with one another.
"Again I say to you, that if two of you agree on earth about anything that they may ask, it shall be done for them by My Father who is in heaven. "For where two or three have gathered together in My name, I am there in their midst." Matthew 18:19-20 (NASB)

Continued ⟶

Prayer

Prayer requires faith and perseverance.
Therefore I tell you, whatever you ask for in prayer, believe that you have received it, and it will be yours. Mark 11:24 (NIV)

Then Jesus told his disciples a parable to show them that they should always pray and not give up. Luke 18:1 (NIV)

Prayer was taught by Jesus to his disciples.
One day Jesus was praying in a certain place. When he finished, one of his disciples said to him, "Lord, teach us to pray, just as John taught his disciples." Luke 11:1 (NIV)

Prayer is God's will for us and to be a continual part of our lives.
Be joyful always; pray continually; give thanks in all circumstances, for this is God's will for you in Christ Jesus.
1 Thessalonians 5:16-18 (NIV)

Prayer is a means for enlightenment among God's people.
I pray also that the eyes of your heart may be enlightened in order that you may know the hope to which he has called you, the riches of his glorious inheritance in the saints, and his incomparably great power for us who believe. Ephesians 1:18-19 (NIV)

Prayer is a means for strengthening.
That according to the riches of his glory he may grant you to be strengthened with power through his Spirit in your inner being, so that Christ may dwell in your hearts through faith—that you, being rooted and grounded in love, may have strength to comprehend with all the saints what is the breadth and length and height and depth, and to know the love of Christ that surpasses knowledge, that you may be filled with all the fullness of God. Ephesians 3:16-19 (ESV)

Prayer of a righteous man is powerful and effective.
The prayer of a righteous man is powerful and effective. Elijah was a man just like us. He prayed earnestly that it would not rain, and it did not rain on the land for three and a half years. Again he prayed, and the heavens gave rain, and the earth produced its crops.
James 5:16-18 (NIV)

Prayer and Laying on of Hands

While the laying on of hands during prayer may appear to be little more than placing a hand on someone else's shoulder, as a biblical and theological practice it is profound.

Laying on of hands was something Jesus did when healing.
When the sun was setting, the people brought to Jesus all who had various kinds of sickness, and laying his hands on each one, he healed them. Luke 4:40 (NIV)

Laying on of hands accompanied Paul's healing.
Then Ananias went to the house and entered it. Placing his hands on Saul, he said, "Brother Saul, the Lord—Jesus, who appeared to you on the road as you were coming here—has sent me so that you may see again and be filled with the Holy Spirit." Acts 9:17 (NIV)

Laying on of hands was something Paul did when healing.
His father was sick in bed, suffering from fever and dysentery. Paul went in to see him and, after prayer, placed his hands on him and healed him. Acts 28:8 (NIV)

Laying on of hands accompanied ordination.
They presented these men to the apostles, who prayed and laid their hands on them. Acts 6:6 (NIV)

So after they had fasted and prayed, they placed their hands on them and sent them off. Acts 13:3 (NIV)

Laying on of hands for ordination should not be done hastily.
Do not be hasty in the laying on of hands, and do not share in the sins of others. Keep yourself pure. 1 Timothy 5:22 (NIV)

Laying on of hands was considered an elementary teaching.
Therefore let us leave the elementary doctrine of Christ and go on to maturity, not laying again a foundation of repentance from dead works and of faith toward God, and of instruction about washings, the laying on of hands, the resurrection of the dead, and eternal judgment. Hebrews 6:1-2 (ESV)

Prayer in the New Testament

They prayed for justice for his people.
Will not God bring about justice for His elect who cry to Him day and night, and will He delay long over them? Luke 18:7 (NASB)

They prayed for boldness in preaching and to save unbelievers.
Brethren, my heart's desire and my prayer to God for them is for their salvation. Romans 10:1 (NASB)

Now, Lord, consider their threats and enable your servants to speak your word with great boldness. Acts 4:29 (NIV)

They prayed for signs and wonders to honor Jesus.
Stretch out your hand to heal and perform miraculous signs and wonders through the name of your holy servant Jesus." Acts 4:30 (NIV)

They prayed for the casting out of demons and raising the dead.
And He said to them, "This kind cannot come out by anything but prayer. Mark 9:29 (NASB)

But Peter sent them all out and knelt down and prayed, and turning to the body, he said, "Tabitha, arise." And she opened her eyes, and when she saw Peter, she sat up. Acts 9:40 (NASB)

They prayed for deliverance from captivity.
But about midnight Paul and Silas were praying and singing hymns of praise to God, and the prisoners were listening to them; and suddenly there came a great earthquake, so that the foundations of the prison house were shaken; and immediately all the doors were opened and everyone's chains were unfastened. Acts 16:25-26 (NASB)

They prayed for church leadership to be established.
When they had appointed elders for them in every church, having prayed with fasting, they commended them to the Lord in whom they had believed. Acts 14:23 (NIV)

Prayer in Tongues

Prayer in tongues is the practice of praying in what sounds audibly like gibberish but is a vocalization enabled by the Spirit of God.

Praying in tongues is a gift given to some by the Holy Spirit.
And in the church God has appointed first of all apostles, second prophets, third teachers, then workers of miracles, also those having gifts of healing, those able to help others, those with gifts of administration, and those speaking in different kinds of tongues.
1 Corinthians 12:28 (NIV)

Those who pray in tongues speak to God, not to men.
For one who speaks in a tongue does not speak to men but to God; for no one understands, but in his spirit he speaks mysteries.
1 Corinthians 14:2 (NASB)

Those who pray in tongues edify themselves.
One who speaks in a tongue edifies himself; but one who prophesies edifies the church. 1 Corinthians 14:4 (NASB)

Prayer in tongues is unintelligible, but still profitable.
For if I pray in a tongue, my spirit prays, but my mind is unfruitful. What is the outcome then? I will pray with the spirit and I will pray with the mind also; I will sing with the spirit and I will sing with the mind also. 1 Corinthians 14:14-15 (NASB)

For others to understand what is being prayed in tongues, there must be an interpretation.
Therefore let one who speaks in a tongue pray that he may interpret.
1 Corinthians 14:13 (NASB)

Using known languages is preferable to tongues in church worship.
I thank God, I speak in tongues more than you all; however, in the church I desire to speak five words with my mind so that I may instruct others also, rather than ten thousand words in a tongue.
1 Corinthians 14:18-19 (NASB)

Prayer in tongues is not to be forbidden.
Therefore, my brethren, desire earnestly to prophesy, and do not forbid to speak in tongues. 1 Corinthians 14:39 (NASB)

Problem of Evil

The philosophical problem of evil is best summarized in the question: "If God is good, then why does he continue to allow evil?" This question is a "problem" in that many draw the conclusion that God is either:

1. Good but unable to stop evil, and thus not all powerful.
2. Able to stop evil, but not in fact good.

Neither of these conclusions are biblically acceptable, as the Bible portrays God as both good and all-powerful. Therefore, there must be another explanation.

The problem of evil is addressed by God's plan to end suffering.
And I heard a loud voice from the throne saying, "Behold, the dwelling place of God is with man. He will dwell with them, and they will be his people, and God himself will be with them as their God. He will wipe away every tear from their eyes, and death shall be no more, neither shall there be mourning, nor crying, nor pain anymore, for the former things have passed away." Revelation 21:3-4 (ESV)

The problem of evil is addressed by Jesus' suffering in our place and for our redemption.
But he was pierced for our transgressions, he was crushed for our iniquities; the punishment that brought us peace was upon him, and by his wounds we are healed. Isaiah 53:5 (NIV)

The problem of evil is addressed in the Spirit's care of Christians while we suffer.
I consider that our present sufferings are not worth comparing with the glory that will be revealed in us. In the same way, the Spirit helps us in our weakness. We do not know what we ought to pray for, but the Spirit himself intercedes for us with groans that words cannot express. And we know that in all things God works for the good of those who love him, who have been called according to his purpose. What, then, shall we say in response to this? If God is for us, who can be against us? He who did not spare his own Son, but gave him up for us all—how will he not also, along with him, graciously give us all things?
Romans 8:18, 26, 28, 31, 32 (NIV)

Remarriage

Remarriage in certain cases was prohibited in the Old Testament, in order to protect women from serial divorce.
If a man marries a woman who becomes displeasing to him because he finds something indecent about her, and he writes her a certificate of divorce, gives it to her and sends her from his house, and if after she leaves his house she becomes the wife of another man, and her second husband dislikes her and writes her a certificate of divorce, gives it to her and sends her from his house, or if he dies, then her first husband, who divorced her, is not allowed to marry her again after she has been defiled. That would be detestable in the eyes of the LORD.
Deuteronomy 24:1-4 (NIV)

Remarriage causes adultery, unless "unfaithfulness" was present in the prior marriage, or one's spouse has died.
But I tell you that anyone who divorces his wife, except for marital unfaithfulness, causes her to become an adulteress, and anyone who marries the divorced woman commits adultery. Matthew 5:32 (NIV)

And I say to you: whoever divorces his wife, except for sexual immorality, and marries another, commits adultery." The disciples said to him, "If such is the case of a man with his wife, it is better not to marry." But he said to them, "Not everyone can receive this saying, but only those to whom it is given. For there are eunuchs who have been so from birth, and there are eunuchs who have been made eunuchs by men, and there are eunuchs who have made themselves eunuchs for the sake of the kingdom of heaven. Let the one who is able to receive this receive it." Matthew 19:9-12 (ESV)

Remarriage is encouraged as a means of reconciliation between those who have divorced one another.
To the married I give this command (not I, but the Lord): A wife must not separate from her husband. But if she does, she must remain unmarried or else be reconciled to her husband. And a husband must not divorce his wife. 1 Corinthians 7:10-11 (NIV)

Remarriage does not cause adultery if there was unfaithfulness in the prior marriage, but neither is it approved due to unfaithfulness.
But I tell you that anyone who divorces his wife, except for marital unfaithfulness, causes her to become an adulteress, and anyone who marries the divorced woman commits adultery. Matthew 5:32 (NIV)

Repentance

Repentance is God's righteous expectation for humanity.
God is a righteous judge, and a God who has indignation every day. If a man does not repent, He will sharpen His sword; He has bent His bow and made it ready. Psalm 7:11-12 (NASB)

Repentance brings salvation.
For thus the Lord GOD, the Holy One of Israel, has said, "In repentance and rest you will be saved, In quietness and trust is your strength." But you were not willing. Isaiah 30:15 (NASB)

Repentance has fruit, and is an indication that God is our Father.
But when he saw many of the Pharisees and Sadducees coming for baptism, he said to them, "You brood of vipers, who warned you to flee from the wrath to come? "Therefore bear fruit in keeping with repentance; and do not suppose that you can say to yourselves, 'We have Abraham for our father'; for I say to you that from these stones God is able to raise up children to Abraham. Matthew 3:7-9 (NASB)

Repentance is the reason Jesus came.
And Jesus answered and said to them, "It is not those who are well who need a physician, but those who are sick. "I have not come to call the righteous but sinners to repentance." Luke 5:31-32 (NASB)

Repentance is a gift from Jesus.
He is the one whom God exalted to His right hand as a Prince and a Savior, to grant repentance to Israel, and forgiveness of sins. Acts 5:31 (NASB)

When they heard this, they quieted down and glorified God, saying, "Well then, God has granted to the Gentiles also the repentance that leads to life." Acts 11:18 (NASB)

Repentance was the message of the early church.
First to those in Damascus, then to those in Jerusalem and in all Judea, and to the Gentiles also, I preached that they should repent and turn to God and prove their repentance by their deeds. Acts 26:20 (NIV)

Continued ⟶

Repentance

Repentance is brought by God's kindness.
Or do you show contempt for the riches of his kindness, tolerance and patience, not realizing that God's kindness leads you toward repentance? Romans 2:4 (NIV)

Repentance is a result of godly sorrow.
For even if I made you grieve with my letter, I do not regret it—though I did regret it, for I see that that letter grieved you, though only for a while. As it is, I rejoice, not because you were grieved, but because you were grieved into repenting. For you felt a godly grief, so that you suffered no loss through us. For godly grief produces a repentance that leads to salvation without regret, whereas worldly grief produces death. 2 Corinthians 7:8-10 (ESV)

Repentance is fueled by godly sorrow produces specific fruit.
See what this godly sorrow has produced in you: what earnestness, what eagerness to clear yourselves, what indignation, what alarm, what longing, what concern, what readiness to see justice done. At every point you have proved yourselves to be innocent in this matter. 2 Corinthians 7:11 (NIV)

Repentance brings escape from the devil's trap.
And the Lord's servant must not be quarrelsome but kind to everyone, able to teach, patiently enduring evil, correcting his opponents with gentleness. God may perhaps grant them repentance leading to a knowledge of the truth, and they may come to their senses and escape from the snare of the devil, after being captured by him to do his will. 2 Timothy 2:24-26 (ESV)

Repentance is what God wants in everyone's life.
The Lord is not slow in keeping his promise, as some understand slowness. He is patient with you, not wanting anyone to perish, but everyone to come to repentance. 2 Peter 3:9 (NIV)

Salvation

Salvation cannot be inherited.
Therefore bear fruit in keeping with repentance; and do not suppose that you can say to yourselves, 'We have Abraham for our father'; for I say to you that from these stones God is able to raise up children to Abraham. Matthew 3:8-9 (NASB)

Salvation comes by God's grace through faith, not by works.
For it is by grace you have been saved, through faith—and this not from yourselves, it is the gift of God—not by works, so that no one can boast. Ephesians 2:8-9 (NIV)

Salvation comes through faith in Jesus Christ.
The jailer called for lights, rushed in and fell trembling before Paul and Silas. He then brought them out and asked, "Sirs, what must I do to be saved?" They replied, "Believe in the Lord Jesus, and you will be saved—you and your household." Acts 16:29-31 (NIV)

Salvation comes only through the person Jesus Christ.
"Salvation is found in no one else, for there is no other name under heaven given to men by which we must be saved." Acts 4:12 (NIV)

Salvation comes as we call upon the name of the Lord.
Because, if you confess with your mouth that Jesus is Lord and believe in your heart that God raised him from the dead, you will be saved. For with the heart one believes and is justified, and with the mouth one confesses and is saved. For the Scripture says, "Everyone who believes in him will not be put to shame." Romans 10:9-11 (ESV)

Salvation is made available through Christ's blood.
Since we have now been justified by his blood, how much more shall we be saved from God's wrath through him! For if, when we were God's enemies, we were reconciled to him through the death of his Son, how much more, having been reconciled, shall we be saved through his life! Romans 5:9-10 (NIV)

Salvation comes through the message of the cross.
For the message of the cross is foolishness to those who are perishing, but to us who are being saved it is the power of God. 1 Corinthians 1:18 (NIV)

Salvation and God's Sovereignty

God's revelation is revealed by Jesus to those he chooses.
"All things have been committed to me by my Father. No one knows who the Son is except the Father, and no one knows who the Father is except the Son and those to whom the Son chooses to reveal him."
Luke 10:22 (NIV)

God's decision brings new birth to those who believe.
Yet to all who received him, to those who believed in his name, he gave the right to become children of God—children born not of natural descent, nor of human decision or a husband's will, but born of God.
John 1:12-13 (NIV)

God draws to Jesus those he wills.
"No one can come to me unless the Father who sent me draws him, and I will raise him up at the last day. John 6:44 (NIV)

God enables us to come to Jesus.
Yet there are some of you who do not believe." For Jesus had known from the beginning which of them did not believe and who would betray him. He went on to say, "This is why I told you that no one can come to me unless the Father has enabled him." John 6:64-65 (NIV)

God foreknew those he will glorify.
For those God foreknew he also predestined to be conformed to the likeness of his Son, that he might be the firstborn among many brothers. And those he predestined, he also called; those he called, he also justified; those he justified, he also glorified. Romans 8:29-30 (NIV)

God predestined us to be adopted as sons through Jesus Christ.
Even as he chose us in him before the foundation of the world, that we should be holy and blameless before him. In love he predestined us for adoption as sons through Jesus Christ, according to the purpose of his will, to the praise of his glorious grace, with which he has blessed us in the Beloved. Ephesians 1:4-6 (ESV)

God must reveal himself to us and save us as we are natural.
The natural person does not accept the things of the Spirit of God, for they are folly to him, and he is not able to understand them because they are spiritually discerned. 1 Corinthians 2:14 (ESV)

Salvation and Our Assurance

Assurance of salvation comes by believing God's promises.
"For God so loved the world that he gave his one and only Son, that whoever believes in him shall not perish but have eternal life.
John 3:16 (NIV)

If we confess our sins, he is faithful and just and will forgive us our sins and purify us from all unrighteousness. 1 John 1:9 (NIV)

Assurance of salvation comes as we keep God's commands.
And by this we know that we have come to know him, if we keep his commandments. Whoever says "I know him" but does not keep his commandments is a liar, and the truth is not in him, but whoever keeps his word, in him truly the love of God is perfected. By this we may know that we are in him: whoever says he abides in him ought to walk in the same way in which he walked. 1 John 2:3-6 (ESV)

Assurance of salvation comes as we produce works of faith.
What good is it, my brothers, if a man claims to have faith but has no deeds? Can such faith save him? In the same way, faith by itself, if it is not accompanied by action, is dead. James 2:14, 17 (NIV)

Assurance of salvation comes by God's testimony in our heart.
We accept man's testimony, but God's testimony is greater because it is the testimony of God, which he has given about his Son. Anyone who believes in the Son of God has this testimony in his heart.
1 John 5:9-10 (NIV)

Assurance of salvation comes by the Spirit's presence in our lives.
Because you are sons, God sent the Spirit of his Son into our hearts, the Spirit who calls out, "Abba, Father." So you are no longer a slave, but a son; and since you are a son, God has made you also an heir.
Galatians 4:6-7 (NIV)

Salvation and Our Perseverance

Perseverance in salvation means standing firm until the end.
All men will hate you because of me, but he who stands firm to the end will be saved. Matthew 10:22 (NIV)

Perseverance in salvation means holding firm to the Gospel.
Now, brothers, I want to remind you of the gospel I preached to you, which you received and on which you have taken your stand. By this gospel you are saved, if you hold firmly to the word I preached to you. Otherwise, you have believed in vain. 1 Corinthians 15:1-2 (NIV)

He has now reconciled in his body of flesh by his death, in order to present you holy and blameless and above reproach before him, if indeed you continue in the faith, stable and steadfast, not shifting from the hope of the gospel that you heard, which has been proclaimed in all creation under heaven, and of which I, Paul, became a minister. Colossians 1:22-23 (ESV)

We have come to share in Christ if we hold firmly till the end the confidence we had at first. Hebrews 3:14 (NIV)

Perseverance in salvation means helping others turn from sin.
My brothers, if one of you should wander from the truth and someone should bring him back, remember this: Whoever turns a sinner from the error of his way will save him from death and cover over a multitude of sins. James 5:19-20 (NIV)

Perseverance in salvation means exalting even in tribulations.
And not only this, but we also exult in our tribulations, knowing that tribulation brings about perseverance; and perseverance, proven character; and proven character, hope; and hope does not disappoint, because the love of God has been poured out within our hearts through the Holy Spirit who was given to us. Romans 5:3-5 (NASB)

Perseverance in salvation means working out our faith.
So then, my beloved, just as you have always obeyed, not as in my presence only, but now much more in my absence, work out your salvation with fear and trembling; for it is God who is at work in you, both to will and to work for His good pleasure. Philippians 2:12-13 (NASB)

Salvation and Our Security

Security in salvation comes through Jesus' promise to lose none.
All that the Father gives me will come to me, and whoever comes to me I will never cast out." John 6:37 (ESV)

Security in salvation comes from Jesus' power and authority.
I give them eternal life, and they shall never perish; no one can snatch them out of my hand. My Father, who has given them to me, is greater than all; no one can snatch them out of my Father's hand.
John 10:28-29 (NIV)

Security in salvation comes through the Holy Spirit's presence.
In Him, you also, after listening to the message of truth, the gospel of your salvation--having also believed, you were sealed in Him with the Holy Spirit of promise, who is given as a pledge of our inheritance, with a view to the redemption of God's own possession, to the praise of His glory. Ephesians 1:13-14 (NASB)

Now He who prepared us for this very purpose is God, who gave to us the Spirit as a pledge. 2 Corinthians 5:5 (NASB)

Security in salvation comes as we believe God's Word.
For those God foreknew he also predestined to be conformed to the likeness of his Son, that he might be the firstborn among many brothers. And those he predestined, he also called; those he called, he also justified; those he justified, he also glorified. Romans 8:29-30 (NIV)

Security in salvation is in Jesus' promise to finish what he started.
Being confident of this, that he who began a good work in you will carry it on to completion until the day of Christ Jesus.
Philippians 1:6 (NIV)

Security in salvation is in Jesus, the author and perfecter of faith.
Let us fix our eyes on Jesus, the author and perfecter of our faith, who for the joy set before him endured the cross, scorning its shame, and sat down at the right hand of the throne of God. Hebrews 12:2 (NIV)

Security in salvation is experienced by those who remain.
They went out from us, but they were not really of us; for if they had been of us, they would have remained with us; but they went out, so that it would be shown that they all are not of us. 1 John 2:19 (NASB)

Satan

Satan means "adversary," but he is also called by names such as: "the devil" (Matthew 4:1), "Beelzebul" (Matthew 10:25), and "the prince of the power of the air" (Ephesians 2:2).

Satan was seen by Jesus falling from heaven.
"I saw Satan fall like lightning from heaven." Luke 10:18 (NIV)

Satan is a murderer and the father of lies, who comes to destroy.
He was a murderer from the beginning, not holding to the truth, for there is no truth in him. When he lies, he speaks his native language, for he is a liar and the father of lies. John 8:44 (NIV)

The thief comes only to steal and kill and destroy; I have come that they may have life, and have it to the full. John 10:10 (NIV)

And no wonder, for Satan himself masquerades as an angel of light. 2 Corinthians 11:14 (NIV)

Satan comes to try and steal God's Word when it is sown.
Some people are like seed along the path, where the word is sown. As soon as they hear it, Satan comes and takes away the word that was sown in them. Mark 4:15 (NIV)

Satan is our enemy and to be resisted.
Be self-controlled and alert. Your enemy the devil prowls around like a roaring lion looking for someone to devour. Resist him, standing firm in the faith. 1 Peter 5:8-9 (NIV)

Satan's work in the world will be defeated by Jesus.
The God of peace will soon crush Satan under your feet The grace of our Lord Jesus be with you. Romans 16:20 (NASB)

"Now the salvation, and the power, and the kingdom of our God and the authority of His Christ have come, for the accuser of our brethren has been thrown down, he who accuses them before our God day and night." Revelation 12:10 (NASB)

Scripture

Scripture denotes the name given to the collection of 66 books making up the Old and New Testaments of the Bible. This book made up of books is a history of God's saving work through Jesus Christ.

Scripture was provided as God spoke through the prophets.
I will raise up for them a prophet like you from among their brothers. And I will put my words in his mouth, and he shall speak to them all that I command him. And whoever will not listen to my words that he shall speak in my name, I myself will require it of him.
Deuteronomy 18:18-19 (ESV)

All Scripture is God-breathed and is useful for teaching, rebuking, correcting and training in righteousness, so that the man of God may be thoroughly equipped for every good work. 1 Timothy 3:16-17 (NIV)

Above all, you must understand that no prophecy of Scripture came about by the prophet's own interpretation. For prophecy never had its origin in the will of man, but men spoke from God as they were carried along by the Holy Spirit. 2 Peter 1:20-21 (NIV)

And we also thank God continually because, when you received the word of God, which you heard from us, you accepted it not as the word of men, but as it actually is, the word of God, which is at work in you who believe. 1 Thessalonians 2:13 (NIV)

The eyes of everyone in the synagogue were fastened on him, and he began by saying to them, "Today this scripture is fulfilled in your hearing." Luke 4:20-21 (NIV)

And beginning with Moses and all the Prophets, he explained to them what was said in all the Scriptures concerning himself.
John 24:27 (NIV)

Scripture's Authority

Scripture's authority is based on the belief that it comes from God.
Knowing this first of all, that no prophecy of Scripture comes from someone's own interpretation. For no prophecy was ever produced by the will of man, but men spoke from God as they were carried along by the Holy Spirit. 2 Peter 1:20-21 (ESV)

Scripture's authority is demonstrated in the command to integrate it into every facet of our lives.
And these words that I command you today shall be on your heart. You shall teach them diligently to your children, and shall talk of them when you sit in your house, and when you walk by the way, and when you lie down, and when you rise. You shall bind them as a sign on your hand, and they shall be as frontlets between your eyes. You shall write them on the doorposts of your house and on your gates. Deuteronomy 6:6-9 (ESV)

Do not let this Book of the Law depart from your mouth; meditate on it day and night, so that you may be careful to do everything written in it. Then you will be prosperous and successful. Joshua 1:8 (NIV)

Scripture's authority is demonstrated in its promise of power.
How can a young man keep his way pure? By guarding it according to your word. With my whole heart I seek you; let me not wander from your commandments! I have stored up your word in my heart, that I might not sin against you. Psalm 119:9-11 (NIV)

Jesus answered, "It is written: 'Man does not live on bread alone, but on every word that comes from the mouth of God.'" Matthew 4:4 (NIV)

Scripture's authority is seen in its usefulness for good works.
All Scripture is God-breathed and is useful for teaching, rebuking, correcting and training in righteousness, so that the man of God may be thoroughly equipped for every good work. 2 Timothy 3:16-17 (NIV)

Scripture's authority is seen in its power to reveal our motives.
For the word of God is living and active and sharper than any two-edged sword, and piercing as far as the division of soul and spirit, of both joints and marrow, and able to judge the thoughts and intentions of the heart. Hebrews 4:12 (NASB)

Continued ⟶

Scripture's Authority

Scripture's authority is seen in that it comes from God's mouth and accomplishes God's purposes.

"For as the rain and the snow come down from heaven, and do not return there without watering the earth and making it bear and sprout, and furnishing seed to the sower and bread to the eater; So will My word be which goes forth from My mouth; It will not return to Me empty, without accomplishing what I desire, and without succeeding in the matter for which I sent it. Isaiah 55:10-11 (NASB)

Scripture's authority is seen in the fulfillment of prophecy.

Then beginning with Moses and with all the prophets, He explained to them the things concerning Himself in all the Scriptures.
Luke 24:27 (NASB)

The Scripture, foreseeing that God would justify the Gentiles by faith, preached the gospel beforehand to Abraham, saying, "ALL THE NATIONS WILL BE BLESSED IN YOU." Galatians 3:8 (NASB)

Scripture's authority is seen in the command that it be preached.

Preach the word; be ready in season and out of season; reprove, rebuke, exhort, with great patience and instruction.
2 Timothy 4:2 (NASB)

Until I come, give attention to the public reading of Scripture, to exhortation and teaching. 1 Timothy 4:13 (NASB)

Scripture's Inerrancy

Scripture's inerrancy is the belief that the Bible is without error in all that it affirms, and thus completely trustworthy and authoritative for our lives. The logic is fairly simple. Because we affirm that the Bible is God's Word and we know that God never lies, then we also know that the Bible never lies. Affirming the Bible's inerrancy is the historic position of Christianity.

Inerrancy does not mean however, that the Bible tells us everything there is to know about the world, but rather that whatever it does say about a subject is always true. In other words, the Bible is true and reliable in all that it addresses and we must work hard to understand what it is, and is not, addressing. For example, it is important to remember that the Bible is not primarily a science book, but rather a history of God's saving work through Jesus.

This means that where the Bible makes particular claims, whether scientific (ex. descriptions of how the natural order works), historic (ex. descriptions of what took place or how many were involved), or mathematical (ex. rounding numbers), certain statements might lack modern precision or accuracy. We must remember that the Bible was not written by or for modern readers, but rather by and for ancient authors and audiences, and we must accept that reality that God worked through ancient authors, who utilized ancient writing standards and methods, in order to reveal himself. Ancient writing standards and methods does not undermine the veracity of the text, but it does require our diligently working to understand ancient writing.

For example, offering variant reports on parallel accounts or topical arrangements of events rather than linear were both accepted practices within ancient history writing. It was also not uncommon for ancient authors to report falsehoods or using hyperbole, which makes it important to remember that God spoke to human authors and worked through their unique personalities, particular writing styles and within their specific cultural settings, to communicate his message. None of which compromises the truthfulness of Scripture.

When there are apparent errors or contradictions within the Biblical text we encourage diligence in study, realizing that all truth is God's truth and that he cannot contradict himself. We also encourage humility in making assertions, admitting that we are finite in our understanding and that collecting more data may change our understanding. Ultimately, to deny inerrancy is to undermine the authority and reliability of Scripture and to make yourself the judge of God's Word.

Scripture's Interpretation

Scripture's interpretation must begin with prayer, inviting God to teach us through the work of the Holy Spirit (John 16:13). Scripture is a unified and understandable whole, accessible to all who seek the truth in faith (Matthew 7:7). Thus, interpreting Scripture includes a commitment to accept the testimony of Scripture at face value, doing our best to read and understand the text as the author intended it to be read.

Second, we should work diligently to accurately interpret God's word (2 Timothy 2:15) and avoid imposing our personal pre-suppositions upon the text. A diligent study should include:

• Reading the passage in context, reviewing the surrounding verses, paragraphs, and chapters, as well as understanding the genre of the book, whether poetry, history, gospel, etc.

• Identifying the author and audience, and understanding their cultural context. The Bible is inspired by God (2 Timothy 3:16), which means God revealed his saving work to ancient audiences through ancient authors. Understanding the cultural context of the ancient world helps understand Scripture's message.

• Researching the grammar used within the passage, looking for any comparisons or contrasts and identifying basic grammatical structures. Noting word usage (i.e. definitions, key words or repeated words or phrases), indications of literal or figurative intent based on the context. Comparing various translations can help gain greater understanding.

• Researching complementary passages of Scripture. The best interpreter of Scripture is Scripture itself. When a passage is particularly difficult to understand make sure to use the Scripture that is clearest to interpret passages that are less clear, as well as explicit passages to interpret the implicit.

Third, we should come believing, possessing a confidence that Scripture has a message for us today. God's Word is unique in that despite being written to ancient audiences by ancient authors, it continues to speak today (Hebrews 4:12).

Scripture's Reliability

Scripture's reliability is seen in God's writing the first commands.
When the LORD finished speaking to Moses on Mount Sinai, he gave him the two tablets of the Testimony, the tablets of stone inscribed by the finger of God. Exodus 20:18 (NIV)

Scripture's reliability rests in God commanding Moses to record certain events.
Then the LORD said to Moses, "Write this as a memorial in a book and recite it in the ears of Joshua, that I will utterly blot out the memory of Amalek from under heaven." Exodus 17:14 (ESV)

Scripture's reliability is seen in its unity despite being written over thousands of years and by many different authors.
Moses came and told the people all the words of the LORD and all the rules. And all the people answered with one voice and said, "All the words that the LORD has spoken we will do." And Moses wrote down all the words of the LORD. He rose early in the morning and built an altar at the foot of the mountain, and twelve pillars, according to the twelve tribes of Israel. Exodus 24:3-4 (ESV)

After Moses finished writing in a book the words of this law from beginning to end, he gave this command to the Levites who carried the ark of the covenant of the LORD : Deuteronomy 31:24-25 (NIV)

And Joshua recorded these things in the Book of the Law of God. Then he took a large stone and set it up there under the oak near the holy place of the LORD. Joshua 24:26 (NIV)

Samuel explained to the people the regulations of the kingship. He wrote them down on a scroll and deposited it before the LORD. Then Samuel dismissed the people, each to his own home.
1 Samuel 10:25 (NIV)

This is the word that came to Jeremiah from the LORD : "This is what the LORD, the God of Israel, says: 'Write in a book all the words I have spoken to you.'" Jeremiah 30:1-2 (NIV)

Continued——▶

Scripture's Reliability

Scripture's reliability was affirmed by Jesus.
And beginning with Moses and all the Prophets, he explained to them what was said in all the Scriptures concerning himself.
John 24:27 (NIV)

Scripture's reliability is rooted in the promise of the Spirit's ministry to teach the apostles and remind them of Jesus' word.
But the Counselor, the Holy Spirit, whom the Father will send in my name, will teach you all things and will remind you of everything I have said to you. John 14:26 (NIV)

But when he, the Spirit of truth, comes, he will guide you into all truth. John 16:13 (NIV)

Scripture's reliability is demonstrated in the apostle's testimony of receiving revelation from the Spirit.
However, as it is written: "No eye has seen, no ear has heard, no mind has conceived what God has prepared for those who love him"—but God has revealed it to us by his Spirit. 1 Corinthians 2:9-10 (NIV)

This is what we speak, not in words taught us by human wisdom but in words taught by the Spirit, expressing spiritual truths in spiritual words. 1 Corinthians 2:13 (NIV)

Scripture's reliability is affirmed by the early church.
Long ago, at many times and in many ways, God spoke to our fathers by the prophets, but in these last days he has spoken to us by his Son, whom he appointed the heir of all things, through whom also he created the world. Hebrews 1:1-2 (NIV)

Continued⟶

Scripture's Reliability

Scripture's reliability rests in the apostle's claim to speak for God.
If anybody thinks he is a prophet or spiritually gifted, let him acknowledge that what I am writing to you is the Lord's command.
1 Corinthians 14:37 (NIV)

Above all, you must understand that no prophecy of Scripture came about by the prophet's own interpretation. For prophecy never had its origin in the will of man, but men spoke from God as they were carried along by the Holy Spirit. 2 Peter 1:20-21 (NIV)

I want you to recall the words spoken in the past by the holy prophets and the command given by our Lord and Savior through your apostles. 2 Peter 3:2 (NIV)

Scripture's reliability is seen in Peter's affirmation that Paul's writings are equal with the other Scripture.
And count the patience of our Lord as salvation, just as our beloved brother Paul also wrote to you according to the wisdom given him, as he does in all his letters when he speaks in them of these matters. There are some things in them that are hard to understand, which the ignorant and unstable twist to their own destruction, as they do the other Scriptures. 2 Peter 3:15-16 (ESV)

Scripture's reliability is seen in Paul quoting Luke's report of Jesus' teaching as authoritative.
For the Scripture says, "Do not muzzle the ox while it is treading out the grain," and "The worker deserves his wages."
1 Timothy 5:18 (NIV)

Scripture's Translation

The books of the Bible were originally written in the ancient languages of Hebrew (Old Testament) and Greek (New Testament), and modern English translations have different strengths, depending upon the priorities of the translators.

Each of the following translations are known as "formal" equivalents, or literal translations, meaning that the original languages were translated word for word into English. Because of the differences between ancient and modern languages, these translations are more stilted and difficult to read. However, what these translations lose in readability, they gain in accuracy. We would recommend these translations to someone wanting to know what the Bible really *says*.

New American Standard Bible (NASB)
New King James Version (NKJV)
English Standard Version (ESV)
Revised Standard Version (RSV)
New Revised Standard Version (NRSV)

The following are known as "functional" translations, meaning that they translate the original languages phrase by phrase into English, which makes them much easier to read. However, what these translations lose in accuracy they gain in readability. We would recommend these translations to someone wanting to know what the Bible really *means*. These are often the preferred translations of newer believers who might be distracted or discouraged from reading if the wording is awkward or cumbersome.

New Living Translation (NLT)
The Message

Between formal and functional translations are those that aim at accuracy and readability. Some examples are:

New International Version (NIV)
Today's New International Version (TNIV)

Service

Service is the reason we were created by God.
For we are God's workmanship, created in Christ Jesus to do good works, which God prepared in advance for us to do.
Ephesians 2:10 (NIV)

Service was modeled by Jesus.
Have this attitude in yourselves which was also in Christ Jesus, who, although He existed in the form of God, did not regard equality with God a thing to be grasped, but emptied Himself, taking the form of a bond-servant, and being made in the likeness of men. Being found in appearance as a man, He humbled Himself by becoming obedient to the point of death, even death on a cross. Philippians 2:5-8 (NASB)

Service was commended by Jesus.
If I then, the Lord and the Teacher, washed your feet, you also ought to wash one another's feet. For I gave you an example that you also should do as I did to you. John 13:14-15 (NASB)

Service is to be accomplished through the gifts of the Holy Spirit.
To each is given the manifestation of the Spirit for the common good.
1 Corinthians 12:7 (ESV)

Service is the work for which Christians are to be equipped.
It was he who gave some to be apostles, some to be prophets, some to be evangelists, and some to be pastors and teachers, to prepare God's people for works of service, so that the body of Christ may be built up. Ephesians 4:11-12 (NIV)

Service is what Christians are to offer one another.
You, my brothers, were called to be free. But do not use your freedom to indulge the sinful nature; rather, serve one another in love. The entire law is summed up in a single command: "Love your neighbor as yourself." Galatians 5:13 (NIV)

Service is the result of using talents with which we are entrusted.
"His master said to him, 'Well done, good and faithful slave. You were faithful with a few things, I will put you in charge of many things; enter into the joy of your master.' Matthew 25:23 (NASB)

Sex

Sex was designed by God to join a husband and wife together.

For this reason a man shall leave his father and his mother, and be joined to his wife; and they shall become one flesh. And the man and his wife were both naked and were not ashamed.
Genesis 2:24-25 (NASB)

Do you not know that your bodies are members of Christ himself? Shall I then take the members of Christ and unite them with a prostitute? Never! Do you not know that he who unites himself with a prostitute is one with her in body? For it is said, "The two will become one flesh." But he who unites himself with the Lord is one with him in spirit.
1 Corinthians 6:15-17 (NIV)

Sex is a means to honoring God with our body.

Flee immorality. Every other sin that a man commits is outside the body, but the immoral man sins against his own body. Or do you not know that your body is a temple of the Holy Spirit who is in you, whom you have from God, and that you are not your own? For you have been bought with a price: therefore glorify God in your body.
1 Corinthians 6:18-20 (NASB)

Sex between those not married is fornication and prohibited.

And He was saying, "That which proceeds out of the man, that is what defiles the man. "For from within, out of the heart of men, proceed the evil thoughts, fornications, thefts, murders, adulteries, deeds of coveting and wickedness, as well as deceit, sensuality, envy, slander, pride and foolishness. All these evil things proceed from within and defile the man." Mark 7:20-23 (NASB)

Therefore it is my judgment that we do not trouble those who are turning to God from among the Gentiles, but that we write to them that they abstain from things contaminated by idols and from fornication and from what is strangled and from blood. Acts 15:19-20 (NASB)

Sin

Sin is any attitude or action contrary to the character of God, as revealed in the Law, as well as a state of being, into which all humanity is born.

Sin entered the world through one man, and death through sin.
Therefore, just as sin entered the world through one man, and death through sin, and in this way death came to all men, because all sinned. Romans 5:12 (NIV)

Sin is any action or attitude contrary to God's character as revealed in the law.
Everyone who sins breaks the law; in fact, sin is lawlessness.
1 John 3:4 (NIV)

Sin is also the state of being into which we are all born.
All of us also lived among them at one time, gratifying the cravings of our sinful nature and following its desires and thoughts. Like the rest, we were by nature objects of wrath. Ephesians 2:3 (NIV)

Sin is the result of our own evil desires.
But each one is tempted when he is carried away and enticed by his own lust. Then when lust has conceived, it gives birth to sin; and when sin is accomplished, it brings forth death. James 1:14-15 (NASB)

Sin and death have been overcome through the death of Jesus.
The Law came in so that the transgression would increase; but where sin increased, grace abounded all the more, so that, as sin reigned in death, even so grace would reign through righteousness to eternal life through Jesus Christ our Lord. Romans 5:20-21 (NASB)

Sin is present with all people, but salvation from sin comes to all who believe in Jesus Christ.
This righteousness from God comes through faith in Jesus Christ to all who believe. There is no difference, for all have sinned and fall short of the glory of God, and are justified freely by his grace through the redemption that came by Christ Jesus. Romans 3:22-24 (NIV)

Spiritual Warfare

Spiritual warfare was a reality for Jesus.
Then Jesus was led by the Spirit into the desert to be tempted by the devil. After fasting forty days and forty nights, he was hungry. The tempter came to him and said, "If you are the Son of God, tell these stones to become bread." Matthew 4:1-3 (NIV)

Spiritual warfare was a reality for the early church.
As we were going to the place of prayer, we were met by a slave girl who had a spirit of divination and brought her owners much gain by fortune-telling. She followed Paul and us, crying out, "These men are servants of the Most High God, who proclaim to you the way of salvation." And this she kept doing for many days. Paul, having become greatly annoyed, turned and said to the spirit, "I command you in the name of Jesus Christ to come out of her." And it came out that very hour. Acts 16:16-18 (ESV)

Spiritual warfare is fought through Jesus' name.
She kept this up for many days. Finally Paul became so troubled that he turned around and said to the spirit, "In the name of Jesus Christ I command you to come out of her!" At that moment the spirit left her. Acts 16:18 (NIV)

The seventy-two returned with joy and said, "Lord, even the demons submit to us in your name." Luke 10:17 (NIV)

Spiritual warfare is won by Jesus' blood and our testimony.
They overcame him by the blood of the Lamb and by the word of their testimony; they did not love their lives so much as to shrink from death. Revelation 12:11 (NIV)

Spiritual warfare should not distract from celebrating salvation.
However, do not rejoice that the spirits submit to you, but rejoice that your names are written in heaven." Luke 10:20 (NIV)

Spiritual warfare is made possible by divinely powerful weapons.
For though we live in the world, we do not wage war as the world does. The weapons we fight with are not the weapons of the world. On the contrary, they have divine power to demolish strongholds. 2 Corinthians 10:3-4 (NIV)

Continued ⟶

Spiritual Warfare

Spiritual warfare is focused on arguments and pretensions.
We demolish arguments and every pretension that sets itself up against the knowledge of God, and we take captive every thought to make it obedient to Christ. 2 Corinthians 10:5 (NIV)

Spiritual warfare is to be fought while wearing God's armor.
Finally, be strong in the Lord and in the strength of his might. Put on the whole armor of God, that you may be able to stand against the schemes of the devil. Ephesians 6:10-11 (ESV)

Spiritual warfare is fought against spiritual forces of evil.
For our struggle is not against flesh and blood, but against the rulers, against the authorities, against the powers of this dark world and against the spiritual forces of evil in the heavenly realms. Ephesians 6:12 (NIV)

Spiritual warfare is fought by self-control and resistance in faith.
Be sober-minded; be watchful. Your adversary the devil prowls around like a roaring lion, seeking someone to devour. Resist him, firm in your faith, knowing that the same kinds of suffering are being experienced by your brotherhood throughout the world. 1 Peter 5:8-9 (ESV)

Spiritual warfare is supported by heavenly forces.
And Elisha prayed, "O LORD, open his eyes so he may see." Then the LORD opened the servant's eyes, and he looked and saw the hills full of horses and chariots of fire all around Elisha. 2 Kings 6:17 (NIV)

Then he said to me, "Do not be afraid, Daniel, for from the first day that you set your heart on understanding this and on humbling yourself before your God, your words were heard, and I have come in response to your words. "But the prince of the kingdom of Persia was withstanding me for twenty-one days; then behold, Michael, one of the chief princes, came to help me, for I had been left there with the kings of Persia." Daniel 10:12-13 (NASB)

Temptation

Temptation is brought by the evil one.
And lead us not into temptation, but deliver us from the evil one.
Matthew 6:13 (NIV)

Temptation can be avoided through prayer.
"Watch and pray so that you will not fall into temptation. The spirit is willing, but the body is weak." Matthew 26:41 (NIV)

Temptations of all types are common and can be escaped.
No temptation has seized you except what is common to man. And God is faithful; he will not let you be tempted beyond what you can bear. But when you are tempted, he will also provide a way out so that you can stand up under it. 1 Corinthians 10:13 (NIV)

Temptation can come while trying to help others.
Brothers, if someone is caught in a sin, you who are spiritual should restore him gently. But watch yourself, or you also may be tempted. Galatians 6:1 (NIV)

Temptation was experienced and resisted by Jesus.
Then Jesus was led by the Spirit into the desert to be tempted by the devil. Matthew 4:1 (NIV)

For we do not have a high priest who is unable to sympathize with our weaknesses, but we have one who has been tempted in every way, just as we are—yet was without sin. Hebrews 4:15 (NIV)

Temptation is never brought by God, or experienced by God.
Let no one say when he is tempted, "I am being tempted by God," for God cannot be tempted with evil, and he himself tempts no one. But each person is tempted when he is lured and enticed by his own desire. Then desire when it has conceived gives birth to sin, and sin when it is fully grown brings forth death. James 1:13-15 (ESV)

Trials and Suffering

Trials and suffering were common for Christ and the disciples.
"You are those who have stayed with me in my trials, and I assign to you, as my Father assigned to me, a kingdom, that you may eat and drink at my table in my kingdom and sit on thrones judging the twelve tribes of Israel. Luke 22:28-30 (ESV)

Trials and suffering were foretold for Christ's followers.
"I have told you these things, so that in me you may have peace. In this world you will have trouble. But take heart! I have overcome the world." John 16:33 (NIV)

Trials and suffering are an opportunity to develop perseverance.
Count it all joy, my brothers, when you meet trials of various kinds, for you know that the testing of your faith produces steadfastness. And let steadfastness have its full effect, that you may be perfect and complete, lacking in nothing. James 1:2-4 (ESV)

Trials and suffering are overcome through the Lord's rescue.
If this is so, then the Lord knows how to rescue godly men from trials and to hold the unrighteous for the day of judgment, while continuing their punishment. 2 Peter 2:9 (NIV)

Trials and suffering were common among the early church.
We sent Timothy, who is our brother and God's fellow worker in spreading the gospel of Christ, to strengthen and encourage you in your faith, so that no one would be unsettled by these trials. You know quite well that we were destined for them. In fact, when we were with you, we kept telling you that we would be persecuted. And it turned out that way, as you well know. 1 Thessalonians 3:2-4 (NIV)

Trials and suffering may be granted to us by God.
For it has been granted to you on behalf of Christ not only to believe on him, but also to suffer for him. Philippians 2:29 (NIV)

Trials and suffering can be endured by God's sufficient grace.
Three times I pleaded with the Lord about this, that it should leave me. But he said to me, "My grace is sufficient for you, for my power is made perfect in weakness." 2 Corinthians 12:8-9 (ESV)

Trinity

That God eternally exists in three persons (i.e. Father, Son and Holy Spirit), with each person being fully God, while at the same time being one in essence is the doctrine of the Trinity. This means that all of God's attributes (ex. eternality, omniscience, omnipresence, etc) are fully present in all three persons of the God-head equally. While difficult to fully understand, Trinitarian theology is essential to the Christian faith.

The Trinity was revealed in the life and teachings of Jesus.
At that moment heaven was opened, and he saw the Spirit of God descending like a dove and lighting on him. And a voice from heaven said, "This is my Son, whom I love; with him I am well pleased."
Matthew 6:16-17 (NIV)

Go therefore and make disciples of all nations, baptizing them in the name of the Father and of the Son and of the Holy Spirit, teaching them to observe all that I have commanded you. And behold, I am with you always, to the end of the age." Matthew 28:19-20 (ESV)

The Trinity is referred to by both Peter and Paul.
May the grace of the Lord Jesus Christ, and the love of God, and the fellowship of the Holy Spirit be with you all.
2 Corinthians 13:14 (NIV)

According to the foreknowledge of God the Father, by the sanctifying work of the Spirit, to obey Jesus Christ and be sprinkled with His blood: May grace and peace be yours in the fullest measure.
1 Peter 1:1-2 (NASB)

The Trinity makes up only one God, with three distinct persons.
For there is one God, and one mediator also between God and men, the man Christ Jesus. 1 Timothy 2:5 (NASB)

You believe that God is one You do well; the demons also believe, and shudder. James 2:19 (NASB)

Wisdom

Wisdom is given by God to all those who ask.
If any of you lacks wisdom, let him ask God, who gives generously to all without reproach, and it will be given him. But let him ask in faith, with no doubting, for the one who doubts is like a wave of the sea that is driven and tossed by the wind. For that person must not suppose that he will receive anything from the Lord; James 1:5-7 (ESV)

Wisdom from God is personified in the person of Jesus Christ.
It is because of him that you are in Christ Jesus, who has become for us wisdom from God—that is, our righteousness, holiness and redemption. Therefore, as it is written: "Let him who boasts boast in the Lord." 1 Corinthians 1:30-31 (NIV)

Wisdom is proven wise in the rightness of its actions.
For John came neither eating nor drinking, and they say, 'He has a demon.' The Son of Man came eating and drinking, and they say, 'Look at him! A glutton and a drunkard, a friend of tax collectors and sinners!' Yet wisdom is justified by her deeds." Matthew 11:18-19 (ESV)

Wisdom begins with fearing God, and results in shunning evil.
"But where can wisdom be found? Where does understanding dwell? And he said to man, 'The fear of the Lord—that is wisdom, and to shun evil is understanding.'" Job 28:12, 28 (NIV)

The fear of the LORD is the beginning of knowledge; Fools despise wisdom and instruction. Proverbs 1:7 (NIV)

"I, wisdom, dwell with prudence, and I find knowledge and discretion. The fear of the LORD is hatred of evil. Pride and arrogance and the way of evil and perverted speech I hate. I have counsel and sound wisdom; I have insight; I have strength.. Proverbs 8:12-14 (ESV)

Work

Work is an activity in which God himself participates.
By the seventh day God had finished the work he had been doing; so on the seventh day he rested from all his work. Genesis 2:2 (NIV)

Work was assigned to mankind in the Garden of Eden.
The LORD God took the man and put him in the Garden of Eden to work it and take care of it. Genesis 2:15 (NIV)

Work became toil and less productive as a consequence of sin.
*And to Adam he said, "Because you have listened to the voice of your wife and have eaten of the tree of which I commanded you, 'You shall not eat of it, 'cursed is the ground because of you; in pain you shall eat of it all the days of your life; thorns and thistles it shall bring forth for you; and you shall eat the plants of the field. By the sweat of your face you shall eat bread, till you return to the ground, for out of it you were taken; for you are dust, and to dust you shall return."
Genesis 3:17-19 (ESV)*

Work is enabled by skills given by God and is for his glory.
The LORD said to Moses, "See, I have called by name Bezalel the son of Uri, son of Hur, of the tribe of Judah, and I have filled him with the Spirit of God, with ability and intelligence, with knowledge and all craftsmanship, to devise artistic designs, to work in gold, silver, and bronze, in cutting stones for setting, and in carving wood, to work in every craft. Exodus 31:1-5 (ESV)

To one he gave five talents of money, to another two talents, and to another one talent, each according to his ability. Then he went on his journey. Matthew 25:15 (NIV)

So whether you eat or drink or whatever you do, do it all for the glory of God. 1 Corinthians 10:31 (NIV)

Work is an expected activity for survival.
For even when we were with you, we gave you this rule: "If a man will not work, he shall not eat." 2 Thessalonians 3:10 (NIV)

Worship

Worship is more than singing songs of praise during a church service. Worship is a lifestyle of giving God the glory and honor due only him. Worship is our response of honoring God for who he is and what he has done through Jesus Christ.

Worship is being sought by God the Father from among people.
But an hour is coming, and now is, when the true worshipers will worship the Father in spirit and truth; for such people the Father seeks to be His worshipers. John 4:23 (NASB)

Worship that God is seeking must be offered in spirit and truth.
God is spirit, and those who worship Him must worship in spirit and truth. John 4:24 (NASB)

Worship of God requires our bodies being offered in sacrifice.
Therefore I urge you, brethren, by the mercies of God, to present your bodies a living and holy sacrifice, acceptable to God, which is your spiritual service of worship. Romans 12:1 (NASB)

Worship is offered through the Spirit and Christ's Word.
Do not get drunk with wine, for that is dissipation, but be filled with the Spirit, speaking to one another in psalms and hymns and spiritual songs, singing and making melody with your heart to the Lord; always giving thanks for all things in the name of our Lord Jesus Christ to God, even the Father. Ephesians 5:18-20 (NASB)

*Let the word of Christ richly dwell within you, with all wisdom teaching and admonishing one another with psalms and hymns and spiritual songs, singing with thankfulness in your hearts to God.
Colossians 3:16 (NASB)*

Worship was received by Jesus Christ while he was on earth.
*As soon as He was approaching, near the descent of the Mount of Olives, the whole crowd of the disciples began to praise God joyfully with a loud voice for all the miracles which they had seen, shouting: "BLESSED IS THE KING WHO COMES IN THE NAME OF THE LORD; Peace in heaven and glory in the highest!"
Luke 19:37-38 (NASB)*

Glossary

Advent. Latin word meaning "coming." Advent celebrates Jesus' birth (Luke 2:16), and the Church awaits the second advent of his return (Acts 1:11).

Agnosticism. The belief that knowledge of God, or knowledge of anything beyond what may be observed, is unknowable.

Atheism. The belief that there are no deities, no supernatural power beyond what we can observe.

Amen. An affirmation of agreement said at the end of prayers or in response to Scripture that means "may it be" (Psalm 41:13).

Amillennialism. The theological view that there will not be a literal reign of Jesus Christ on earth for a thousand years before the final judgment. Those holding this view interpret Revelation 20 as describing our present church age.

Antichrist. The "man of lawlessness" appearing prior to Jesus' return and bringing great sin and suffering (2 Thessalonians 2:13).

Apocrypha. A collection of books included with the Bible by the Roman Catholic Church, but not considered as equal to the testimony of Scripture.

Arianism. A heresy denying the full deity of Jesus Christ and the Holy Spirit.

Ark of the Covenant. A box used by the Israelites to carry the Ten Commandments, Aaron's rod and a jar of manna. It was a symbol of God's presence among his people (Exodus 25:10-11).

Ascension. Refers to Jesus Christ's departure into the heavens. Because he had been raised from the dead, when he left the earth he went up into the sky (Acts 1:9-11).

Ash Wednesday. The Wednesday that begins Lent, and is observed by placing a small bit of ashes on one's forehead as a symbol of repentance (Luke 10:13).

Atonement. To "pay" for sin through sacrifice (Romans 3:25).

Charismatic. From the Greek *charisma*, meaning gift, most often refers to those who practice the gifts of speaking in tongues, healing, etc. as listed in 1 Corinthians 12-14. This theology gained renewed popularity in the 1960's and 1970's in America, but is distinct from Pentecostalism in that they do not hold that one must speak in tongues as an evidence of salvation.

Catechism. From the Greek word *katecheo*, meaning to instruct, this is formalized system of Bible training. Augustine and Martin Luther both wrote catechisms, and parents are instructed to teach their children (Ephesians 6:4).

Cessationist. The belief that certain spiritual gifts (ex. speaking in tongues and healing) ceased with the first apostles.

Christmas. The celebration of the birth of Jesus Christ (Luke 2).

Common Grace. God's gracious care and kindness toward all people (Matthew 5:45), which is distinct from his "special" grace revealed to those who are being saved (Matthew 11:25).

Compatibilism. The Reformed theology that teaches God's sovereignty is compatible with man's freedom to make real choices (Philippians 2:12-13).

Covenant. Any binding agreement that establishes a relationship. God entered a covenant with Abraham (Genesis 15:18). Jesus Christ was the fulfillment of God's agreement with Abraham and the beginning of the new covenant (Luke 22:20, Hebrews 8:6).

Creed. A formal statement of belief. The Bible contains several early creeds (Philippians 2:1-11; Timothy 3:16), and several were written by early Christians (Apostle's Creed, Nicene Creed).

Docetism. A heresy that denied Jesus' full humanity (Hebrews 4:15).

Doctrine. A truth or system of truths from Scripture (1 Timothy 4:6).

Doxology. A combination of the Greek *doxa*, which means glory, and *logos*, which means word, this is a short hymn of praise to God.

Easter. The celebration of the resurrection of Jesus Christ (Luke 24).

Ecclesiology. From the Greek *ekklesia*, meaning assembly, this is the study of the Church and its function (Ephesians 3:10).

Egalitarian. The belief that all functions and roles are open to men and women alike (Galatians 3:28). This view is the opposite of complementarianism, which teaches that while men and women are equal in worth and value they have distinct roles and responsibilities in church leadership (1 Timothy 2:12).

Eschatology. From the Greek *eskhatos*, meaning last things, this is the study of end times and things.

Election. God choosing individuals to receive salvation through faith in Jesus Christ (Romans 9:11).

Eucharist. From the Greek *eucharistia*, meaning thanksgiving, this is the meal of remembrance established by Jesus Christ on the night before his death, also known as Communion or the Lord's Supper (1 Corinthians 11:17-34).

Evangelical. From the Greek *evangelion*, which means good news, this term describes anyone who believes the gospel is the "power of God for salvation" (Romans 1:16) and makes it a priority to proclaim the gospel.

Exegesis. The activity of interpreting and applying a passage of the Bible. Often includes grammatical and historical studies.

Ex Nihilo. Latin phrase meaning "out of nothing," referring to God's creative work in Genesis 1, in which he used no previously existing materials.

Fundamentalism. Strictly adhering to essential beliefs. Originally referred to a theologically conservative response to liberal theology of the early 20th century, the "fundamentals" included an affirmation of the Bible's inspiration and inerrancy and the historical reality of the miracles reported in the Bible.

Gap Theory. The belief that a large gap in time exists between Genesis 1:1 and Genesis 1:2, during which God judged an earlier creation, making it "formless and empty" (Genesis 1:2), and clearing the way for another creative act as described in balance of Genesis 1.

General Revelation. Knowledge of God's existence revealed to all through creation (Romans 1:20).

Gloria in Excelsis Deo. The title of a well-known Christmas carol this Latin phrase means "Glory to God in the highest," and is quote taken from the angels who met shepherds in the field on Christmas Eve (Luke 2:14).

Glorification. The third and final step in process of salvation. Following justification and sanctification, glorification is the culmination of receiving new bodies and being perfected in righteousness (Romans 8:30).

Good Friday. The Friday before Easter, commemorating Jesus' crucifixion.

Great Commission. A command of Jesus to his disciples, just before his ascension, to go and make more disciples (Matthew 28:18-20).

Great Tribulation. The period of tremendous suffering prior to the return of Jesus Christ (Matthew 24:21).

Hallelujah. Transliteration of the Hebrew word meaning "praise."

Heresy. A teaching or practice that denies one or more essential Christian beliefs such as the deity of Christ or the inherent sinfulness of humanity.

Heretic. One who teaches or practices any denial of one or more essential Christian beliefs such as the deity of Christ or the inherent sinfulness of humanity (1 Timothy 1:20).

Hermeneutics. The theory and/or rules governing biblical interpretation and application.

Heterodox. Any teaching or practice at variance with the historic orthodox teachings and practices of Christianity. Heterodoxy often leads to heresy.

Hypostatic Union. From the Greek *hypostasis*, meaning substantive reality, this is a technical term describing the unique union of Jesus Christ's humanity and divinity (John 1:1, Hebrews 1:3).

Imputed Righteousness. The transfer of Jesus Christ's righteousness to those who believe in his death and resurrection for salvation (Romans 5:12-17).

Imputed Sin. The transfer of sin from the first humans, Adam and Eve, to all of humanity (Romans 5:12). The good news of the Gospel is that just as sin is transferred from Adam and Eve to all humanity, the righteousness of Jesus Christ is transferred to all who believe (Romans 3:22). This is the theological principle of "imputation."

Justification. The doctrine that God declares sinners to be "just" on the basis of faith in Jesus' death (Romans 3:24-26).

Kenosis. From the Greek *kenoo*, which means emptied, this word refers to the activity needed for God, as Jesus Christ, to become fully man, while maintaining his deity (Philippians 2:7).

Lent. The 40 day period of repentance, beginning with Ash Wednesday, and ending with Easter Sunday.

Logos. The Greek term translated as "word" in John 1:1. The term was understood in the ancient world to represent the creative, governing and unifying principle of reason that sustains all of creation.

Maranatha. A ancient Aramaic word beckoning Jesus' urgent return (1 Corinthians 16:22).

Maundy Thursday. Also known as Holy Thursday, it is the Thursday before Easter, commemorating the Last Supper of Jesus (1 Corinthians 11:23-26).

Mercy Seat. The cover, or lid, made of gold that was on top of the Ark of the Covenant. On top of the mercy seat were two gold statues of Cherubim, which are heavenly beings. Once a year, on the Day of Atonement, the blood of from a bull was sprinkled on the mercy seat, as the people sought God's forgiveness for sins committed (Leviticus 16:11-19).

Millennium. A thousand years, most often designating the period of Jesus' reign on earth, whether literal or figurative (Revelation 20:1-7).

Modalism. The heretical teaching that denies the Trinitarian teaching that God exists in three distinct persons, but rather that he simply appears in different modes.

Monergism. A combination of the Greek words *mono*, which means one, and *erg*, which means work, refers to the belief that the Holy Spirit is the singularly active agent in regeneration.

Nestorianism. A heresy during the fifth century that taught there were two separate persons in Christ, one human and one divine, which is contrary to the orthodox teaching that the person of Jesus was at one and the same time both fully God and fully man.

New Testament. The 27 books that make up the second major portion of the Bible, recording the ministry of Jesus Christ, as a fulfillment of Old Testament prophecy, and the beginning of the Church.

Occult. A term that refers to "hidden" or "secret" knowledge, which is beyond ordinary human knowledge. In an effort to discover this hidden knowledge occultists may attempt to speak with the dead, or cast spells, etc. These activities are condemned in the Bible (Deuteronomy 18:10).

Old Testament. The 39 books of the Hebrew Scripture, which make up the first portion of the Bible. These books record the history of God's relationship with the Hebrew people, and foretell of a God's plan to send a Savior.

Omnipotence. The doctrine that God possesses all power and is able to accomplish all that he desires (Hebrews 1:3).

Omnipresence. The doctrine that God does not have a body and is able to be everywhere at once (John 4:24)

Omniscience. The doctrine that God knows all (1 John 3:20).

Original Sin. The doctrine that all humanity is inherently corrupted by the sin of the first humans, Adam and Eve (Romans 5:12). The good news of the Gospel is that just as sin is transferred from Adam and Eve to all humanity, the righteousness of Jesus Christ is transferred to all who believe (Romans 3:22). This is the theological principle of "imputation."

Orthodoxy. A combination of the Greek words *ortho*, which mean right, and *doxa*, meaning opinion, this term refers to the historically approved beliefs within the Christian faith.

Orthopraxy. A combination of the Greek words, *ortho*, which means right, and *praxis*, which means deed or action, this terms refers to historically approved actions within the Christian faith.

Panentheism. The heretical belief that God is *in* everything that has been created, that he permeates and penetrates all things.

Pantheism. The heretical belief that the universe *is* God and/or that everything in the universe is a part of God.

Parousia. A Greek term referring to someone coming or someone's presence, which is used in reference to the future arrival of Jesus Christ. (Acts 1:11).

Palagianism. A theological heresy named after Pelagius (354-440 AD), denying the doctrine of original sin and teaching that man is able to save himself through good works.

Passover. A meal commemorating the Jewish exodus from Egypt and God's slaying the first born of Egypt but "passing over" the houses marked with blood (Exodus 11). Jesus' shed blood for sin is a type of Passover sacrifice (1 Corinthians 5:7), savings the lives of those marked with it.

Pentecost. From the Greek word meaning "fiftieth." For Jews it is a feast day, known as the Feast of Weeks, coming fifty days after the Passover (Exodus 34:22), and celebrating the first fruits of harvest season. For Christians it is the day that marks the beginning of the Church, when the Holy Spirit descended upon the first disciples (Acts 2:1-4).

Pentecostalism. A denomination that was birthed in the American revival of 1901, and believes that the a subsequent baptism in the Holy Spirit is needed after one is born again, and teaches that speaking in tongues as a necessary evidence of saving faith.

Pietism. A movement within the Lutheran denomination during the 17th and 18th centuries that called for individual discipline in pursuit of holiness.

Polytheism. The heretical belief in many different gods and/or goddesses.

Postmillennialism. The view that Jesus will return after a golden "millennial age" in which the Church makes significant advances in the world with the Gospel.

Predestination. God determining and assuring who will be saved by faith in Jesus Christ (Ephesians 1:11).

Premillennialism. The belief that Jesus will return after the great tribulation, raising Christians who have died from the dead and glorifying the bodies of Christians who are alive, to establish a thousand year reign on earth (Revelation 20:2-7).

Propitiation. The doctrine that God's wrath toward sin was appeased through Jesus' death (Romans 3:25, 1 John 2:2, 4:10), making possible our forgiveness by grace through faith.

Protestant. That branch of Christianity that separated from the Catholic Church as a result of the Protestant Reformation.

Protestant Reformation. A reforming movement that broke from the Catholic Church and aimed at correcting doctrinal error and abuses of power. It began in 1517 with the Catholic priest, Martin Luther, and resulted in the birth of Protestantism.

Purgatory. The place in which Roman Catholic doctrine teaches souls of Christians are held for further purification before going on to heaven.

Rapture. The biblical teaching that Christians living when Jesus Christ returns will be "taken up" into air to meet Jesus (1 Thessalonians 4:17).

Reformed Theology. Often considered synonymous with Calvinism, and best represented in the Westminster Confession, this theology emphasizes the sovereignty of God in salvation.

Regeneration. Refers to the moment one is born again, coming alive spiritually through the life giving presence of the Holy Spirit (Titus 3:5).

Righteousness. Attitudes and actions in keeping with God's character (Psalm 26:6; Isaiah 64:6; Romans 3:10). When justified by God's grace through faith in Jesus Christ, his righteousness is "imputed" to us, that is to say counted as ours (Romans 3:22).

Sacrament. A ceremony instituted by Jesus Christ and observed by the church as a visible sign of salvation (ex. baptism and communion).

Sanctification. Means literally to "set apart." The doctrine of God's work to set apart his people in holiness (Romans 6:22).

Sola Fide. Latin term meaning "faith alone." A phrase from the Protestant Reformation denoting that we are saved only by faith in Jesus Christ's death and resurrection.

Sola Gratia. Latin term meaning "Grace alone." A phrase from the Protestant Reformation denoting that we are saved only by God's grace, contributing nothing and receiving unmerited favor.

Sola Scriptura. Latin term meaning "Scripture alone." A phrase from the Protestant Reformation denoting Scripture's sufficiency and clarity for salvation.

Soli Deo Gloria. Latin term meaning "glory to God alone." A phrase from the Protestant Reformation denoting that we are to live only for God's glory.

Solus Christus. Latin term meaning "Christ alone." A phrase from the Protestant Reformation denoting Jesus Christ's sufficiency as Savior and the only mediator between God and man.

Son of God. A title used by Jesus (Mark 13:32) and others (John 20:31) to designate his equal nature with God.

Son of Man. A title used by Jesus to describe himself as the Savior and fulfillment of Old Testament prophecy (Mark 14:61-62; Daniel 7:13).

Soteriology. From the Greek *soteria*, meaning salvation, this is the study of God's saving work through Jesus Christ.

Synoptic Gospels. Term used to refer to three of the four gospels (i.e. Matthew, Mark, Luke), because of the similarity in style.

Theistic Evolution. The belief that God used evolution in his work of creation.

Transubstantiation. The Roman Catholic doctrine that the bread and wine of Communion literally becomes the body and blood of Jesus.

Yahweh. Personal name of God, appears as "LORD" in most English Bibles, and "Jehovah" in some older translations. Formed from a transliteration of four consonant letters in the Hebrew language, YHWH.